BE M

Raymond Brown w
College until 1986, a
ister of Victoria Baptist Church, Eastbourne. A
frequent speaker at major Christian conven-
tions, he is the author of *The Bible Book by
Book*, which was selected for inclusion in
W. H. Smith's special Easter promotion of
religious titles in 1991.

BE MY DISCIPLE

Following Jesus
in a Secular World

RAYMOND BROWN

Marshall Pickering
An Imprint of HarperCollins*Publishers*

Marshall Pickering is an Imprint of
HarperCollins*Religious*
Part of HarperCollins*Publishers*
77–85 Fulham Palace Road, London W6 8JB

First published in Great Britain
in 1992 by Marshall Pickering

1 3 5 7 9 10 8 6 4 2

A catalogue record for this book is
available from the British Library

ISBN 0 551 02653 7

Phototypeset by Intype, London
Printed and bound in Great Britain by
HarperCollinsManufacturing, Glasgow

Contents

GROWING AND GOING

WHEN JESUS BEGAN his public ministry, the first thing he did was to enlist a team of key workers. These disciples, as they were called, were an extraordinarily diverse group of men, drawn from very different walks of life, but Jesus gathered them together because he wanted them, immediately, as partners in his work and, ultimately, as the nucleus of a new believing community, the Church.

His choice of *twelve* was deliberate. That number was specially important for the Hebrew people, and had moments of significant history behind it. From their earliest days, "twelve" had vividly conveyed their vision of unity, completeness and solidarity. The Jewish people traced the beginning of their corporate life as a nation to Abraham's descendants, the twelve tribes each led by one of Jacob's sons (Genesis 49). With the emergent life of the young Church that number "twelve" continued to be important. The sad vacancy caused by the disloyalty and suicide of Judas had to be filled as soon as possible (Acts 1:15–26) so that, once again, twelve men could shoulder the responsibilities which Christ had entrusted to them. This significant number "twelve" continued to speak to them of their cohesive unity in Christ (Revelation 21:12, 14, 16, 21).

The word "disciple" means "learner". In Old Testament times some of the great prophets gathered a group of followers around them, men who were eager to treasure the prophetic message, often in difficult times, and pass it on to the next generation. We know that Elisha had such a group of "learners" in the ninth century BC, the "sons" or "company of the prophets" (2 Kings, chapters 1–9). In the following century, Isaiah was instructed to "bind up the testimony and seal up the law" among his disciples (Isaiah 8:16). In New Testament times, John the Baptist also had his disciples (Luke 7:18; John 1:35; 3:25), some of whom transferred their allegiance to the Lord Jesus (John 1:36–37). It was natural, therefore, for Christ to draw together a group of helpers to share in his work.

After the Ascension, the use of the name "disciple" began to be extended far beyond the initial twelve followers of Christ. Luke regularly used it in the Acts of the Apostles to describe all those first-century people who committed their lives to the service of Jesus.

Each of the four gospels provides us with a substantial amount of information about how Jesus taught and trained these men, and such passages are of immense importance to us as we explore the discipleship-theme in relation to our life in late twentieth-century society. The discipleship-teaching of the New Testament is specially significant in our day because of two serious perils within the life of the contemporary Church – the dangers of superficiality and insularity. If the disciple's faith is to make any meaningful impact in our modern Western culture, it needs to be both deepened and shared.

Variations on those two themes are found in many of

the discipleship stories in the gospels. To explore them all would take us way beyond the limits of what is possible in a book like this, and we have therefore narrowed the range of material down to one gospel, that of John, and to three disciples who are introduced within its pages – Andrew, Philip and Nathanael.

John probably compiled his gospel after the other three had completed theirs. He knows of a wide range of relevant material which has been at his disposal, but which he has consciously omitted. Throughout his task, he has operated on the principle of judicious selection. He tells us that his aim in editing the material has been to bring his readers to the point of believing commitment based on intelligent theological understanding: "Jesus did many other signs in the presence of his disciples, which are not recorded in this book. But these are written that you may believe that Jesus is the Christ, the Son of God, and that by believing you may have life in his name" (20:30–31).

With the exception of the account of Andrew's response to Christ's call, all the narratives about these three disciples (and the teaching given to them) are found only in John's gospel. It is clear, then, that John's selection of these stories about Andrew, Philip and Nathanael, and the things he said to them, must be of special spiritual importance. We meet those three men in John's opening chapter. It is likely that he wants to use them throughout his gospel to present some key aspects of discipleship-teaching. These passages do not simply describe three New Testament partners of Jesus; they vividly portray vital aspects of Christian discipleship in every generation. From these stories we shall see that the New Testament teaching about discipleship is the only corrective for superficial or nominal Christianity. This is a vital theme in our generation when it is not easy for Christians to "swim against the tide" and maintain their high standards of spirituality and morality in a world where such things are summarily dismissed or openly ridiculed.

It is crucially important also in this Decade of Evangelism that we guard against insular Christianity, which is preoccupied with self-protective patterns of spiritual life, and has little or no concern about those millions of people in our world who do not know Christ. From the stories of Andrew, Philip and Nathanael, brilliantly presented by John in his gospel, we shall see that our Christian discipleship needs to be constantly deepened and vigorously shared. In the following chapters we shall often meet these two mutually dependent themes of spirituality and evangelism, but we start with Andrew, who clearly had things to learn and share about both.

2

FIRST THINGS FIRST

THESE FIRST DISCIPLES were certainly drawn together into a working team, but the Lord Jesus also dealt with them personally. He recognized their specific weaknesses, shared their individual problems, encouraged their distinctive gifts and recognized their special qualities. Naturally, they had to be trained to live and work together as a group, but there were times when he deliberately focused his loving attention on their personal needs. That ought to be a great encouragement to every Christian. In other words, although he calls us to himself for worship, fellowship, teaching, prayer and service (Acts 2:42–47) within the corporate life of his people, that does not mean that we are not *individually* important to him. He knows everything there is to be known about us, and that fact is often underlined in these discipleship-stories.

So, let's begin by looking at the things we can learn from Christ's encounters with Andrew. From the stories in John's gospel three things can be said about him: he was a responsive, responsible and resourceful disciple.

A responsive disciple

We first meet Andrew in the company of Jesus' cousin, John the Baptist. John began his unique ministry in the Judean desert by calling the men and women of his nation to repentance. He was a very special figure, rather like the last of the Old Testament prophets. Those great men sometimes used unforgettable visual aids to press home the urgency of their message. For example, warning his contemporaries about the approaching judgment, Isaiah walked through the streets of Jerusalem scantily dressed like a homeless refugee (Isaiah 20:1–4). In his day, that was a far more arresting way of conveying the message than by using a thousand words. Later, Jeremiah smashed an earthenware jar in a public place so that the people ducked as shattered pieces went flying in all directions (Jeremiah 19:1–13). As the crowd stood there, witnessing this strange behaviour and listening to the prophet's words, they came to realize only too well that he was portraying the disintegration of the nation, the southern kingdom, soon to be scattered in all directions by the threatened and inevitable Babylonian invasion. As part of that exile-experience which followed, Ezekiel used similar pictorial forms to communicate unwelcome truths to his contemporaries (Ezekiel 4:1–5, 17; 12:1–20).

Similarly then, John the Baptist also used this form of "prophetic symbolism" (as the scholars describe it) to portray the essential washing away of the people's sins. In his day it was pointedly radical symbolism for, until that time, the only people to be baptized by immersion in water were Gentiles who wanted to be ceremonially admitted to the Jewish faith by this act of "proselyte baptism" as it was called. In other words, when John urged his contemporaries to come to the Jordan river for baptism, he was telling them in effect that because of their sinful, disobedient lives, they were as far away from God as the most distant Gentile sinner. All their undoubted privileges had not got them very far (Luke 3:7-9).

Among the thousands who listened to this serious and persuasive exposure was a young fisherman from Capernaum, Andrew, son of Zebedee. He responded to John's urgent message and was so eager to learn more that he gave up fishing for a while in order to become one of his disciples. Many great truths he had heard since a boy in synagogue came home to him with renewed appeal now that he was away from the boats and the nets.

But on one particular day (John 1:29-34) it seemed as though all this arresting and relevant Old Testament type of teaching came suddenly and dramatically to remarkable fulfilment. Andrew could never forget that day or the special one that followed it.

Andrew was alongside John when, suddenly, the teacher urged the people to look at a man who was gently making his way through the pressing crowd. As John saw and recognized his cousin coming towards him, he said three things to the people that were impressed for ever on Andrew's memory. They seemed to bring together everything that John had been talking about over the previous weeks and months. He identified Jesus publicly as God's Lamb, as the giver of God's Spirit and as God's Son. These three great truths are at the very heart of the message which, eventually, Andrew took up for himself, and during his lifetime came to share with thousands of others. They are vital truths for us and must stand right at the beginning of any exposition of New Testament discipleship. We cannot possibly be the disciples of Jesus unless we have learnt these three key truths and have come to appropriate them for ourselves: Jesus is the Lamb, gives the Spirit and reveals the Father.

First, *Jesus is the Lamb*. "Look," John said, "the Lamb of God who takes away the sin of the world." What he was saying, in language every Jewish hearer would clearly understand, is that in order to bear or carry our sins away, Jesus is our substitute and our sacrifice.

The people remembered that when the Israelite people were slaves in Egypt, God provided a unique way for their miraculous escape. On a given night, the angel of death would visit every home in the entire Egyptian nation. Although given constant warnings, their Pharoah, or king, had stubbornly refused to release the Hebrew slaves, and God knew that they would only do what he was demanding if they were subject to divine wrath. Every first-born son in all their spiritually-resistant households would die during the night, and only after such a drastic act of judgment would the Israelites be allowed to go. But to distinguish each Jewish household, a perfect lamb had to be slain and its blood sprinkled on the doorframes of every Israelite home (Exodus 12). That night every believing home held the first Passover meal; it was to be kept as a special festival every year to remind these people of their redemption, their deliverance from slavery and oppression. When John the Baptist introduced Jesus to his contemporaries as the Lamb of God, many of them would think immediately of the lamb in their history that they knew best, that lamb in Egypt offered by every household. Every lamb was like a substitute. The lamb died so that the first-born son might not die. The lamb died in his place.

Some of them would also think of another reference to a sacrificial lamb, this time drawn from the prophecy of

Isaiah (52: 13–53:12), from the famous words used to describe the Servant of the Lord: "He was led like a lamb to the slaughter" and "the Lord has laid on him the iniquity of us all". That lamb certainly bore sin or "took it away" as John the Baptist put it. The language was direct and unforgettably moving: He "carried out sorrows". He "took up our infirmities". He was "pierced for our transgressions" and was "crushed for our iniquities". Here again, the lamb was both sin-bearer and sacrifice, and the words which describe him so eloquently in Isaiah 53 can only find their perfect fulfilment in Jesus.

Moreover, John's identification of Jesus was as the Lamb of God whose substitutionary sacrifice would be for the "sin of the world", not just the Jewish people. John knew from his study of the Scripture and his contact with Jesus that his saving death was for all nations, a truth which Andrew never forgot. He remembered it specially on a day, later in the ministry of Jesus, when some Greek worshippers came looking for Jesus. Andrew remembered taking them to Christ, and he vividly recalled what Jesus said to them and to the others who were standing there that day. He told them about his death and said, "But I, when I am lifted up from the earth, will draw *all men* to myself" (John 12:20–33).

The second truth which John shared with Andrew and the others on that special day in the Judean desert was that *Jesus gives the Spirit*. Although for John the very thought of it was overwhelming, Jesus had travelled from his home in northern Galilee right down to the Jordan river specially to be baptized in water by John. He had no sins to confess but wanted more than anything to show men and women what was important for them if they were to live righteously for God. When John confessed that he himself was the unworthy sinner who ought to be baptized by Christ, the Lord Jesus insisted on being baptized. It was a pattern for others to follow: "Let it be so now; it is proper for us to do this to fulfil all righteousness" (Matthew 3:15).

But, important as that baptism was, John knew that every believer would receive another baptism from Jesus himself. John the Baptist spoke forcefully of the contrast: John's baptism was in Jordan's waters, but Christ's baptism would be nothing other than total immersion into the life and power of the Holy Spirit. John was spelling out the truth, and Andrew was carefully taking it in, that every believer who trusts in the substitutionary and sacrificial work of the Lamb of God will, like Jesus, receive the empowering life of God's Holy Spirit. Andrew did not miss the point. Only Jesus would be the giver of the Spirit:

"The man on whom you see the Spirit come down and remain is he who will baptize with the Holy Spirit" (John 1:33).

When, a few years later, Andrew's gifted brother, Peter, preached to the crowds at the great Pentecost festival in Jerusalem, he said much the same thing about the Lord Jesus: "Exalted to the right hand of God, he has received the promised Holy Spirit and has poured out what you now see and hear" (Acts 2:33). Every Christian needs the assurance that in Christ the sacrificial lamb, our sins are carried or taken away as John the Baptist promised. We also need the further truth that, once cleansed and forgiven, we all receive, as Peter said, "the gift of the Holy Spirit" (Acts 2:38).

Andrew came to see that the Spirit was not given to a favoured few, as in Old Testament times, but to all who believed. "The promise is for you and your children and for all who are far off" (Acts 2:39), Peter said, those far and near, Jews and Gentiles, men and women, young and old, masters and servants. This "pouring out" on all of the Holy Spirit was promised by the prophet Joel centuries before Pentecost, and at that festival the disciples of Jesus witnessed the fulfilment of that great prediction. But all of them knew that this new, inward, dynamic presence of the Spirit was the gift of the ascended Christ, and they all rejoiced in the unbelievable transformation which totally revolutionized all their lives.

The third truth which Andrew learnt that day as a disciple of John the Baptist was that *Jesus reveals the Father*. John did not only identify Jesus as the Lamb of God but spoke persuasively of him as "the Son of God" (John 1:34). Here in the presence of all the people in the Judean desert was none other than the unique son of the Father. John had exercised his faithful ministry merely as a "voice", and was content to be just that (John 1:22–23). He never claimed to be anything else. Offended by his honest and forthright teaching, the religious leaders of his day had urged him to identify himself. The religious hierarchy in Jerusalem sent special messengers to ask him who he claimed to be. Was he the Christ, the anointed One (for that is the meaning of the word), the Messiah who was to come? Or was he the prophet Elijah who centuries earlier had ascended to heaven and who, in the intervening years, had come to be endowed in popular thinking with supernatural qualities? Or was he the promised Prophet of Deuteronomy 18:18 who was to be like Moses, raised up among his brothers?

John replied by telling them that he was none of these. He had claimed to be nothing other than a voice, faithfully announcing the coming of someone far greater than himself. That infinitely superior figure was standing unrecognized somewhere in the crowd, said John, but neither identified or acknowledged by the religious leaders of his day: "among you stands one you do not know" (John 1:26). John told them and others who were standing near that he himself did not know Jesus as God's unique Son until the Father revealed it to him: "the one who sent me to baptize with water told me" (John 1:33).

The disciple, Andrew, knew that his teacher John was making a most important point here. Nobody can know the true identity of Jesus until the Father clearly points out his Son to us, and similarly nobody knows the Father until the Lord Jesus reveals him to our spiritually unenlightened minds. John told the crowds with persuasive certainty: "I have seen and testify that this is the Son of God."

The remaining chapters of John's gospel are crammed with further verbal and visual "evidence" of that unique sonship. There are great sayings from the lips of Jesus that persuade convincingly those who, like John, come to believe in him. Jesus constantly spoke of God as "my Father" and told his disciples that "No-one comes to the Father except through me" (John 14:6).

But it is not only what Jesus says which convinces his disciples. The subsequent pages of the gospel also present the reader with convincing "signs" of his sonship, dramatic visual demonstrations that the one who had come into the world to be its Saviour was none other than the Son of God. Who else could heal the sick, feed the hungry, restore sight to the blind, raise the dead? John's "signs" are more than spectacular miracles; they are a convincing demonstration of Christ's deity. That is why the Pharisees wanted to kill Jesus. The more he performed signs of the kind he did at the grief-stricken home in Bethany, the more the people were believing in his deity. Delay was dangerous; the number of his followers was increasing daily, and he must be pursued, arrested and killed.

Once Andrew had grasped these three great truths from the lips of John the Baptist he knew that he must leave the company of John's followers and ask if he might be numbered among the disciples of Jesus. If Jesus was the saving Lamb, the giver of the enabling Spirit and the unique revealer of the Father, then he wanted to be at Christ's side for ever. The very next day Jesus again passed by as John was speaking, and immediately John once more pointed him out to the crowd as "the Lamb of God" (John 1:35–36). Andrew knew that his moment had come. He left John and followed Jesus. It was the beginning of a new relationship as a disciple of Christ. He had responded to John's preaching. All who wish to follow Jesus in their own lives must hear again those three truths which captivated Andrew's mind and compelled him to transfer his allegiance from John to Jesus. He has become a near-perfect example of the responsive disciple, earnestly appropriating every new truth, eager not only to know more about Christ but to apply these truths to everyday living.

Are we now responding to all that we know of Jesus, or is there a disappointing gap between what we *know* intellectually and what we *are* spiritually?

A responsible disciple

But Andrew was not only responsive; he was responsible too. After he had only spent one full day with Jesus, he went to find his own brother, Peter, to bring him to Christ as well. In John's gospel we read that the "first thing" that

Andrew did was to seek out his brother so that he might tell him about Jesus. What is the *first thing* in your life and mine? The very first thing that entered Andrew's newly-arrested mind was the thought that his brother did not know about those three things. He longed not only to share those truths with him but also bring him personally to Christ. Christians of earlier generations used to talk about having "a passion for souls". They meant that the first thing in their lives was the work of personal evangelism. They could not be happy unless their contemporaries were brought to personal faith in the Saviour. Paul described that agonizing priority as "great sorrow and increasing anguish" (Romans 9:2) in his heart, or to use J. B. Phillips' fine paraphrase of those words, it was, the apostle said, "like a pain that never leaves me".

William Temple was right when he described the Church of Christ as "the only organization on earth which exists for the benefit of those who are not yet its members." The Church is like no other society in the world. Groups and clubs of all kinds exist primarily in order to help their members. They join together in activities which promote and further their knowledge of their special interest. Imagine a tennis club whose primary concern was for every non-tennis player in the local community, or a poultry club which aimed to speak personally to everyone in the locality who had no interest whatever in poultry. Can you imagine a golf club where its members could not rest until they had said something about their favourite sport to every non-golfer in the town? The idea sounds ridiculous, but it perfectly describes what should be "the first thing" in the life of every local Church and every individual believer.

Christian history is packed with the stories of those men and women whose "first thing" in life was to bring others to Jesus. Most of them were people who never attained any kind of fame either during their lifetime or since, but they were content to have been used to bring famous people to their Saviour. Let's recall a few of these magnificent "first thing" people.

The name of William Carey is known the world over as the pioneer of the modern missionary movement. His book *The Enquiry* was used to stimulate concern for lost and unreached millions all over the world. Carey's strenuous and persistent efforts among Baptist people led ultimately to the formation of the Baptist Missionary Society, the first of several missionary organizations founded at the end of the eighteenth century and soon after. The great missionary enthusiast was only brought to Christ because a young fellow-apprentice, John Warr, made it "the first thing" in his young life to tell his friend Carey about the Lord Jesus. Reflecting on those early days, Carey wrote:

"*He became importunate with me*, lending me books . . . which gradually wrought a change in my thinking, and my inward uneasiness increased." Carey's biographer says that "John Warr was the Andrew who first led this Peter towards Christ."

Or think of young Anthony Ashley Cooper, later Lord Shaftesbury, brought up in an aristocratic home, but an extremely unhappy one, with little love except that shown to him by Maria Milles. Maria was a servant in the Ashley Cooper household. She belonged to Christ and for her, the "first thing" was to show the love of Jesus to the young boy in her care. All through his later life, Lord Shaftesbury traced the beginnings of his Christian experience to her love and her faithfulness to the Gospel. Every night, before the young boy went to bed, Maria told him stories from the gospels and shared with him the message of Christ's love. Lord Shaftesbury wore to the end of his life a gold watch that she left him in her will, saying that it had once belonged "to the best friend I ever had". On many occasions he told his friends how Maria Milles had urged him as the greatest of life's priorities 'to seek the kingdom of God', and not rest until he had found it".

There was a day in the life of Andrew when he listened to his brother Peter addressing a vast crowd at Pentecost. Andrew must have marvelled at the carefully ordered argument, the ease with which his brother moved from one biblical reference to the other, the persuasive intensity which characterized the whole sermon, its Christ-honouring themes, and its earnest evangelistic appeal. He could not possibly have preached it, but neither would his brother have done so if telling Peter about Jesus had not been the "first thing" which Andrew did when he came to Christ.

A resourceful disciple

But many Christians are honest enough to confess that although they know that personal evangelism ought to be the "first thing" in their lives, they find it hard to open their mouths when the moment of opportunity comes. They feel tongue-tied or embarrassed or unusually sensitive about causing offence, or frightfully unconfident or hesitant about whether they will do it well. Feeding others with the bread of life seems a difficult and demanding assignment and they scarcely know how to begin. It's important for us to remember that huge enterprises often have modest beginnings. This brings us to one of the most famous Andrew stories in John's gospel (6:1–15).

It was the time when the crowds were following Jesus in huge numbers to hear his magnetic preaching and see for themselves the signs he was revealing as he healed the sick. When Jesus saw the vast multitude of people coming across the countryside he asked one of his disciples, Philip, where they might obtain enough bread to satisfy the needs of these hungry people. Philip looked at the crowd, roughly estimated its size, did his sums and came up with a sum of money that would not be enough to meet the cost of only a bite each. Philip outlined what could not be done. At that moment Andrew spoke up; he explained what might be possible: "Here is a boy with five small barley loaves and two small fish, but how far will they go among so many?"

In some ways Andrew is almost as pessimistic as Philip, but there is a touch of the realist about him too. He is more eager to tell Jesus about the loaves they have rather than the money they don't have. Philip can only tell Jesus what won't go round. Andrew at least points to the tiny lunch in the boy's hands. Then with the lad's eager approval, the slender meal is quietly transferred from the boy's hands to the Lord's. In his gospel, John tells us that the Jewish Passover Feast was near. It was a moment for recalling miracles and remembering mercy. It was a day for anticipating help. Not long after the celebration of that first Passover, the Israelite people had been fed in the desert (Exodus 16), thousands of them, not once but for decades. In the hands of Jesus, it happened again. The bread was broken, empty hands were stretched out in need, and the hungry were fed with good things.

For Christian people across the centuries, the miracle has become a parable. It has spoken persuasively to them of the limitless sufficiency of Christ. Whether we are called to personal evangelism, practical service, compassionate help, or anything else, the little we have must be placed submissively into the hands of Christ, totally surrendered to him. He can take it and transform it, as he did the boy's lunch, into food for a multitude.

What a remarkably trusting boy that lad must have been. Most healthy boys love their food, and the prospect of that lovingly prepared lunch must have cheered the lad throughout the long morning as he followed with the crowds, eager to hear what Jesus had to say. Then, suddenly, a disciple is drawing Christ's attention to this meagre meal, and a moment comes when he can let it out of his hands into Christ's. For a boy it was no little sacrifice. Losing the bread, he could be hungry. Once broken, and passed through the hands of others, the tiny loaves might be little more than useless crumbs. But it was not a time for questioning, only for giving, and the lad let it go. Thank God for thousands who, across the centuries, have done exactly the same. They have sacrificially given their money whilst others clutched their possessions. They have offered their time when others have squandered it on useless pursuits. They have surrendered their lives when others have satisfied themselves or pleased themselves, or protected themselves. What a profound mercy that they have been willing to obey the word of Jesus about discipleship, that they have been ready to surrender life rather than save it, and in letting it go have made the same discovery as the young boy on the day the multitude were fed.

He would not have believed it possible. As he made his long way home at the end of the day, the lad saw people carrying baskets, laden with bread and fish, leftovers from the miraculous meal. In all the villages round about, hungry people were dipping gratefully into those large baskets, proving for themselves the reality of Christ's words to his followers: "Give, and it will be given to you. A good measure, pressed down, shaken together and running over will be poured into your lap. For with the measure you use, it will be measured to you" (Luke 6:38). Time and again Christ's people have witnessed what the boy saw that day with astonished eyes, their little made much in the hands of Jesus; that is true Christian resource-fulness.

Jesus said as much to Andrew and his friend Philip on the day they brought some Greek worshippers to meet their Lord (12:20–26). He told the two disciples and the Greek enquirers that sacrifice lies at the heart of all service: "Unless a grain of wheat falls into the ground and dies, it remains only a single seed. But if it dies, it produces many seeds. The man who loves his life will lose it, but the man who hates his life in this world will keep it for eternal life." And following him meant walking the way of the cross, the way of self-giving. The broken bread would for ever speak of life's costliest offering. The priceless grain of a beautiful life would be buried in a tomb. But the fruit would be both abundant and eternal. Jesus was not calling his disciples to anything he was not doing himself. The Incarnation was an immense sacrifice, leaving the glory of heaven for the squalor of earth. The Atonement was doubly so, experiencing the anguish of that sin-bearing death that we might live for ever.

There is, of course, a uniqueness about his sacrifice which dwarfs ours. But once we have accepted the incom-parable merit of his death, it begins to provide a pattern for our life: "Whoever serves me must follow me." Like Andrew, Christ's disciples have witnessed miracles of undeserved mercy as their meagre gifts have been abundantly multiplied in the service of others.

Tradition has it that Andrew ended his days as a missionary in southern Greece and that, in time of fierce local persecution, he was crucified in Achaia. We cannot be sure if that was so, but Andrew of all people would have acknowledged that he too must be willing to let the grain of wheat fall into the ground and die. The seventeenth-century Spanish artist Murillo portrayed on canvas "The Martyrdom of St Andrew". It was an inspired touch to include in the scene, half-turning away in distress, a young boy with tears in his eyes. It captured something of the unpayable debt which must have been felt by an unnamed lad in the hills of Galilee. It poignantly recalled the day when Andrew had taken a boy by the hand and led him into the presence of Jesus. The little that he had was miraculously multiplied. In a wide variety of different ways, the story has been re-enacted in every period of Christian history. Throughout the centuries, disciples have proved that life's essential resources are found in the outstretched hands of Christ.

3

NEVER GIVE UP

NOW THAT WE HAVE LOOKED AT some of Andrew's experiences, we must turn to see what we can learn from his friend Philip. On several occasions in the gospels, two disciples are found together in the same story. Zebedee's sons, James and John, often appear side by side, and the same can also be said of Andrew and Philip. The call of both men to discipleship is found in the same section of the fourth gospel's opening chapter. Later, Andrew and Philip are placed alongside each other as the two spokesmen at the miraculous feeding of the multitude and, later still, they are both responsible for taking those Greek worshippers into the presence of Jesus (John 1:40–41, 43; 6:5–9; 12:20–22).

These two men were brought up in the same city. John makes sure that we know that, for he mentions it twice in his gospel (John 1:44; 12:21). Bethsaida was an interesting place to live. Situated at the northern end of the Sea of Galilee, it had been built by Philip the tetrarch who made it his capital. Although some Jewish people lived in Bethsaida, the tetrarch's region was mainly Gentile territory, and was greatly influenced by Greek culture. Both

Andrew and Philip have Greek names, rare among the
disciples. The presence of large numbers of non-Jews as
their neighbours may have inspired the missionary enthusiasm of both Andrew and Philip. Both men are models of
evangelistic zeal.

That is certainly the main thing which strikes us when
we look carefully at the Philip story. Like Andrew, he is
an eager personal evangelist. But we need also to remember
that he is one evangelist among many in John's gospel.
The theme of effective personal witnessing is a dominant
one in "John". Within its pages we are introduced to a
wide range of people who, in different ways are used to
bring men and women to personal faith in Jesus. There
are at least eight of them in the gospel and in a striking
manner they illustrate different aspects of the personal
evangelist's work: John the Baptist (1:29–37), Andrew
(1:40–41), Philip (1:43–46), the Lord Jesus himself
(3:1–4:27), the Samaritan woman (4:28–42), the blind
man (9:1–34), Lazarus (12:9–11, 17–19) and John himself
(20:31).

These people are specially important for us in this
Decade of Evangelism. Many Christian people are genuinely and rightly concerned about the steady drift away
from the churches in this century, yet an incalculable range
of vastly different people are contacted every single day
by evangelical Christians. Stories in this gospel which
describe the witnessing skills of these eight evangelists are
of great practical importance for us in our late twentieth-
century world.

For our part we must concentrate in this chapter on
Philip, the young convert who becomes the ardent evangelist. Although he is one among many in the fourth gospel,
his enthusiastic work is specially worthy of our careful

attention. He reminds us of four important things in witnessing: we must be grateful, specific, informed, and resilient.

Be grateful

Jesus left the Judean desert where he had met John the Baptist, and made his way back to Galilee. As soon as he got back on his home territory he began to recruit other disciples. He "found" Philip, the man from Bethsaida, and simply said "Follow me". Those two words, "found" and "follow" are at the heart of the evangelist's message. Inspired by those two profound themes of finding and following, Philip becomes a fervent and effective evangelist. "Finding" emphasizes the divine initiative; "following" indicates the human response. He has been "found" by Christ and, determined to follow him, goes out to "find" others. Just as Andrew found his brother Peter (1:41), so Philip goes out to find his friend Nathanael. But it all begins with the sense of abundant gratitude.

Philip goes out to find Nathanael, grateful for *the initiative of Jesus*. He can only find others because he himself has already been found by Jesus. It is this gospel's profoundly simple way of declaring that Christianity does not consist of what we do for God but what he has done for us. Every Christian's story begins in the heart and activity of God. Philip is grateful that Christ has taken the first step by confronting him with his loving, persuasive initiative, and things can never be the same. Philip can go to others because Christ has come to him.

Moreover, Philip is grateful for the *directness of Jesus*. At their very first meeting, he is not confronted with a complicated code of religious obligations or ceremonial directions; he is simply told to follow. That required immense trust because the man or woman who responds has no idea where "following" will lead them to, but they must either do what Jesus says or refuse to go with him. It is not only demanding in its requirement; it is personal in its appeal. At that moment the call to "follow" is addressed to Philip, nobody else. For all his faults, failings, sins and weaknesses, Jesus wants him personally, and says so. The words of the Iona Community hymn capture it memorably:

> Will you come and follow me
> if I but call your name?
> Will you go where you don't know
> and never be the same?
> Will you let my love be shown,
> Will you let my love be known,
> Will you let my life be grown
> in you and you in me?
>
> Lord your summons echoes true
> when you but call my name.
> Let me turn and follow you
> and never be the same.
> In your company I'll go
> where your love and footsteps show.
> Thus I'll move and live and grow
> in you and you in me.[1]

Philip is inspired to win others for Jesus. Moreover, he is given not only the desire but the power to do so. He knows that, in the search for Nathanael, Christ has gone ahead of him. The best personal evangelist believes that when he goes out to "find" a friend, he is simply following in the footsteps of Jesus, the one who is already searching for potential disciples like Nathanael.

It is that sense of astonished wonder which motivates the effective personal soul-winner. Karl Barth put it perfectly: "What He has done for us is not just something which applies to us and is intended for us, a proffered opportunity and possibility. In it He has actually taken us, embraced us, as it were surrounded us, seized us from behind and turned us back again to Himself."[2] With an immense sense of unpayable debt, such people eagerly reach out for others. They know what God has done for them and cannot wait until they have seen him do the same for others. It is the personal directness of the Gospel which drives them out in grateful witnessing.

Disciples like Philip do not engage in personal witnessing because they like it or enjoy it; at times they may find it particularly difficult, even unrewarding, but they do it because they cannot forget the Lord's totally undeserved mercy for them, mercy which he can convey persuasively through them as well as to them.

But the emphasis on gratitude might suggest that evangelism is primarily aimed at expressing and capturing the emotions. The Philip story reminds us, however, that it is not simply a matter of experiencing the blessings of an overflowing heart. The emotional aspect of our faith may inspire us to share the message but the will must also be stirred to go out and speak to a particular individual. A biblically-based evangelistic strategy will also appeal to the volitional element in us as well as the emotional.

Be specific

Philip knows someone who may well respond to the loving initiative of this good news, a deeply spiritual man who could be an immense blessing to others if he became a follower of Jesus. What is interesting is that Philip knows of a definite person to approach. His new-found evangelistic zeal is practical, personal and precise. It is not a pious, indulgent, glowing emotion, dreaming of winning the whole world. His missionary-ministry is not concerned with vague generalities, or unattainable fantasies, nor does it hover in a meaningless void of distant intentions. He is not preoccupied with unattainable missionary ambitions. Philip's enthusiasm is essentially functional. One man comes into his mind; for the time being all others fade. Nathanael is the one person he must find first and tell him about Jesus.

A great deal of well-intended evangelistic enthusiasm evaporates into thin air simply because it fails to be specific. It rarely narrows down to a particular individual. One Saturday morning in mid-nineteenth-century America, an exceptionally shy and reserved Sunday School teacher made his way from his lodgings in Boston to Holton's shoe-store specially to speak to a young eighteen-year-old who was wrapping shoes at the back of the shop. There had been a mission at the Mount Vernon church, and Edward Kimball longed that the young man from his Bible class might trust in Christ. Kimball nearly didn't make it. When he got near to the store, he began to worry whether it was right to be going on such an errand during the lad's working-hours but, under a sense of irresistible compulsion, he "determined to make a dash for it and have it over at once". "I went up to him", said Kimball, "and put my hand on his shoulder . . . I asked him to come to Christ, who loved him and who wanted his love and should have it."

"It seemed that the young man was just ready, for the

light broke upon him, for there, at once, in the back of that shoe store" the young man "gave himself and his life to Christ."

The youth in the back of the shop was Dwight L. Moody, later to become the "Billy Graham of the nineteenth century". As a famous evangelist, Moody would have given anything to have remembered himself exactly what Kimball said to him that unforgettable Saturday morning when he was converted, but he couldn't. Only one thing remained; he remembered that Kimball had tears in his eyes.

As that Sunday School teacher agonized over going to see the young Moody, he could never for a moment have imagined that the Lord was using him to lead to the Saviour someone who, in the years ahead, was to bring many thousands of others to Jesus. Kimball had other young men in his class, but on that Saturday morning he was specific about one. For that moment only one mattered, the lad God had laid specifically on his heart. For nearly a year Moody had sat in Kimball's class, and had listened every week to the preaching of the church's pastor, Edward Norris Kirk, but there had been no visible response. That morning was "the time of God's favour" (2 Corinthians 6:2); what a wonderful thing that on that Saturday Edward Kimball did not indulge in distant dreams of winning all his class for Christ, but obeyed the prompting of God's Spirit to go to see one of them and urge him to accept the Saviour.[3]

A couple of years ago, the church I serve as minister benefited greatly from the Bible Society/Scripture Union video course "Person to Person". I derived enormous help from it, and the thing which made a lasting impression on me was the way the course encouraged us all to think of individuals we ought to reach for Christ. It compelled us to think carefully about particular men and women we met at work or college or at the school-gate, along the street or in the local shop. We were invited to put down their names, begin praying for them, invite our Christian friends to do the same, and think carefully about precise opportunities we might take to share our faith with them – in personal conversation, through a home Bible Discovery group, the use of good literature and so on. The boon of the course was that we not only learned how (and how not!) to witness, but how important it was also to think of specific people we might reach, as Kimball thought of Moody and as, centuries earlier, Philip had thought of Nathanael.

But there is yet something else which is necessary, in addition to the ministry of heart and will – the mind must also be engaged in this best of all tasks. With a grateful heart and practical turn of mind, Philip is determined to seek out one man, a highly intelligent friend. He will do well to think carefully about what he is going to say as he starts this conversation; in this case it will be wise to begin by addressing a key issue, and one which will make a direct appeal to Nathanael's keen and alert mind.

Be informed

Nathanael loved the Old Testament. Jesus said he knew all about Nathanael while he was still "under the fig tree" (1:48), words which were sometimes used by the Jewish people to describe a diligent rabbi studying the Law in the privacy of his own home. Philip therefore begins by speaking about something which will make an immediate appeal to his spiritually literate friend. He talks about the Scripture. If Nathanael is to be led to Christ, he must first see Jesus as the unique fulfilment of God's Word. Otherwise he will dismiss him as another upstart pseudo-Messiah, pretentiously offering the Israelite people deliverance from the Roman oppressor (Acts 5:36–37). Philip begins by asserting that Jesus has come in order to fulfil in detail the predictions of God's unique Word. As a disciple who has himself been "found" by Christ, Philip tells his friend that Christ is to be "found" within the pages of the Bible he knows so well:

"We have found the one Moses wrote about in the Law, and about whom the prophets also wrote" (John 1:45).

Philip's evangelism made its first direct appeal to God's written Word, and to Jesus as the central figure of that book. The Bible is the personal evangelist's unique authority as well as his constant inspiration. The centrality of Scripture is as vital in our own day as it was when Philip first shared his personal faith. In the first century, scores of novel religious ideas were jostling for acceptance by men and women in a wide variety of life's contexts. "Salvation" was a word in common everyday parlance. But salvation from what, and for whom, and by what means? In our own day new religions are proliferating at an alarming rate, and it is virtually impossible to keep up with them. A recently-offered university extra-mural course claimed that there are 500 new religions in Britain today and many of these are to be found throughout Western Europe. In addition to the familiar nineteenth-century sects like Jehovah's Witnesses, Christian Scientists, Mormons and Theosophists (to name but a few), we now have the Baha'i Faith, the Unification Church (or the Moonies), the Church of Scientology, the Children of God or Family of

Love, Herbert Armstrong's Worldwide Church of God with its *Plain Truth* magazine, the Divine Light Mission, and now, more recently, New Age, with others, still emerging, equally weird, spiritually misleading, even damaging.

The new religions appear to make a direct appeal to many people in our late-twentieth-century Western culture. This may well be due to a series of factors, but the phenomena cannot be lightly dismissed. There is a modern rebellion against the use of reason, an emphasis of self-divinization (prominent in New Age thinking, for example), and a wide range of other features. Some of them appear to be looking for slaves rather than disciples, but one thing is certain, they are a prominent aspect of contemporary culture and they cannot be ignored.

Ours is a religious scene not unlike the early Christian centuries with their competing claims for the average man's spiritual allegiance, a world of rival religious attractions such as Gnosticism, Roman Mithraism (an exclusivist "men only" sect, favoured by the Roman army), the so-called "Mystery Religions" with their secret rites and ceremonies, the Emperor worship of the Roman empire, Neoplatonism, Oriental cults, the strange notions of Manichaeism, which at one period proved so strangely attractive to the great Augustine, and so one could go on. It was into that sort of world that the Gospel was preached with such conviction, clarity, and appeal. What was of the greatest importance in that kind of society was to have recourse to the documents of antiquity. Christian evangelists were eager to prove that the message was not an overnight novelty, but was firmly based on a body of reliable teaching, the Hebrew Scriptures, with the testimony of the centuries behind it. In the early Christian centuries, what was "new" was suspect; it was important, therefore, not only to convince Jewish people about Christ from their own Scriptures but to point Gentiles as well to an authentic Book from a reputable literary past.

The Christ "whom Moses wrote about" was the one who had been publicly identified by John the Baptist, none other than the Lamb of God from the Passover narrative of Exodus 12. He was the unique Healer "lifted up" for the salvation of sinful, dying people (like the bronze serpent in the wilderness, John 3:14), the Prophet of Deuteronomy who would share everything the Father had given to him (Deuteronomy 18:18).

The one "about whom the prophets also wrote" was Isaiah's "Suffering Servant" (52:12–53:12), Jeremiah's "Righteous Branch" (23:5), Daniel's "Son of Man" (7:13–14), Zechariah's "Smitten Shepherd" (13:7) and the "Fountain opened for sin and uncleanness" (13:1).

Like Philip, we must base our personal evangelistic opportunities on the clear teaching of Scripture. People are not interested in our personal religious ideas. They need to be pointed not to what we think but to what God has said, plainly and unmistakably in his Word. Every believer needs to know the basic facts of biblical truth – how deeply God longs to meet human need, how destructive sin is in the life of every man and woman, why we need to turn from it, what provision God has made for our deliverance from its penalty and power, why Jesus came into the world, why he died, how we may receive him, what are the consequences of our disobedience, how we can know that those who trust him belong to him for ever.

But, although Philip began his witness by identifying with Nathanael's main interests, there was no reason for him to imagine that his friend would thereby welcome what he had to say. In his brief, arresting opening sentence he started by mentioning the Scripture, but he went on to exalt the Saviour and, immediately he mentioned the name of Jesus, Nathanael became embarrassed, cynical, even annoyed. Those who take Christ's name upon their lips must be prepared for reproach. We must be prepared to carry on, even though we are dismissed, mocked or ridiculed. These discipleship-stories call us to resilient witnessing.

Be resilient

There was almost a sneer on the face of Nathanael when Philip said that Jesus was from Nazareth, "the son of Joseph". Nathanael belonged to Cana, a nearby Galilean village, and his swift retort, "Nazareth! Can anything good come from there?" may be little other than gentle banter which one must expect from any local person about a neighbouring community. In Nathanael's view, Nazareth was a nothing-place. To claim to come from a town like that was a non-event. But there is probably more to it than social superiority. It is likely that Nathanael was speaking from a religious rather than a social perspective. Philip claimed to be introducing him to the Messiah and the Scriptures linked the promised Christ to specific locations, clearly identifiable on a map. Bethlehem had certainly been quoted way back in the eighth century by Micah, but Nazareth! Why, the place is not so much as mentioned anywhere at all in the Old Testament. Few biblically literate people amongst Nathanael's contemporaries would have disagreed with the later verdict of the Pharisees, "a prophet does not come out of Galilee" (7:52).

For a so-called prophet to admit that he came from there was tantamount to destroying his own religious credentials.

Nathanael was mildly scornful, but Philip was undeterred. "Come and see", said the new disciple. His brief reply to his friend's derision reminds us of the importance of a buoyant response when people are eager to put us off, or change the subject, or quick to silence us, or forbid further mention of the topic. On such occasions, the disciple must be sensitive to the right kind of response – smile warmly, breathe deeply, and recognize that another day may well herald a better opportunity. It is certainly not the time to launch a verbal missile, but neither is it the time to give up. Another occasion might produce a different reception. The disciple waits prayerfully, believing it will come.

From a human point of view, my friend Paul Ariga would never had been won for Christ if the disciples around him had been easily put off. Now Paul is one of Japan's leading evangelists, a man whose ministry has been widely used not only in his own country but also in other parts of the Far East. He was brought to the Saviour at the age of sixteen, and I close this chapter by recalling his story because of what it says about three Christians who were ready to persist when they might naturally have been discouraged. On the night of Paul's conversion these three people were, in different ways, used to lead that young Buddhist teenager into the presence of Christ. All three were superbly resilient when they might have given up.

The first disciple was an enthusiastic Christian teenager who confronted Paul Ariga whilst he was on his way to the local Temple on New Year's Eve. That is the time when Buddhist people go to pray for release from their sins, and young Paul had made up his mind to go that night, greatly burdened by a sense of unrelieved guilt. On New Year's Eve the priest sounds the bell 108 times in hope of expiating the 108 sins of which Paul and other Buddhists are supposedly guilty. But this zealous young Japanese believer was determined to get young Paul to a Christian meeting that New Year's Eve and would not be deterred, even using his newly acquired jujitsu skills to get him to the house-meeting. Paul did not want to go and, struggling, made that abundantly clear. But the young Christian refused to be deflected from his purpose. He longed that his schoolfriend should listen that night to the joyous message of Christ's assured forgiveness, not the useless, mournful tolling of a temple bell, and he succeeded. By not giving up, he had played his part in God's plan.

The second resilient disciple was the man in whose home the meeting was to be held. Hideo Nakamura is a Christian tailor who had moved to Shirakawa in north-eastern Japan soon after his home and business had been destroyed by bombs during World War II. He had been away from his home, delivering a suit elsewhere in Tokyo, on the day the bombs fell, and returned to find a huge pile of rubble where once his house had stood. Searching frantically among the debris he found his seriously wounded wife holding up, by her arched back, the heavy weight of concrete and timber to protect her baby daughter lying helplessly beneath her. Quickly trying to rescue them both, her husband noticed that the blood seemed as if it was oozing through the pores on his wife's forehead. Even as he tried to release her, Mr Nakamura thought about Jesus in the Garden of Gethsemane, when "his sweat was like drops of blood falling to the ground" (Luke 22:44). Hideo Nakamura lost his wife but kept his daughter, a little girl saved by the sacrifice of her mother. How easily that Christian tailor, smitten by sorrow, might have given up but, in his grief, he refused to be embittered. He moved to north-eastern Japan to start life afresh, continuing his Christian witness by holding meetings in his new accommodation. It was to that home that Paul Ariga was taken on New Year's Eve. That night Mr Nakamura gave his testimony, speaking with quiet persuasiveness of the merciful goodness of a loving God.

The third resilient disciple was Karl Gustaffson, a Scandinavian missionary who had been compelled to leave his treasured work in China when the Communists took over. At the time of the evacuation he was over 60 years of age; there was every reason for him to bring his missionary career to a close and return to his home in Sweden. But he refused to give up. He had settled in Japan just three years before that New Year's Eve and, with insufficient time to master an intricate language, he spoke over those few years with the aid of an interpreter. The Lord gave him a wonderful text for the closing word of exposition on the night Paul Ariga was brought in, weighed down by his transgressions: "Take heart, son; your sins are forgiven" (Matthew 9:2). That New Year's Eve, Paul Ariga trusted Christ.

On some occasions during the Japan Keswick Convention, Paul has been my interpreter. As I have admired his rich spirituality and benefited from his great gifts of communication, I have thanked the Lord for the resilience and buoyancy of those three contemporary disciples who, at different points in their Christian lives, were undaunted when others might easily have been discouraged.[4]

Philip was like that. He did not argue with Nathanael

either about the status of Nazareth, or the reputation of Joseph, or the lineage of the Messiah, or anything else. That day Nathanael was certainly in a quarrelsome mood, but Philip refused to be drawn into profitless argument. "Come and see" he said, and that was all. At that moment, Nathanael was given the grace to do what his friend had suggested and, as the puzzled enquirer walked toward Christ, the disciple's role was over. Within minutes his friend was face to face with Jesus, and in the presence of Christ all his hostility melted away. In the search for souls, disciples must be ready for the occasional rebuff, or touch of harsh mockery. They remember that Jesus told his men more than once that "following" in his steps was not likely to be easy. There came a day in Philip's life when he heard Jesus say just that: "Whoever serves me must follow me; and where I am my servant also will be." Jesus is often in the place of ridicule and rejection, and his disciples will never be far away.

1 *Heaven shall not wait*, Iona Community, Glasgow 1987
2 Karl Barth, *Church Dogmatics*, Vol IV: The Doctrine of Reconciliation, Part 1, Edinburgh 1956, 88–89
3 John Pollock, *Moody without Sankey*, 1963, 22–25
4 Paul Ariga's story, and that of other Japanese Christians, is vividly told in Ron Heywood, *Japanese Jewels*, Lutterworth Press 1989, 117–19

4

ALMOST PUT OFF

AFTER THE FIRST EASTER, during one of those special times when the Risen Christ kept meeting his followers, he said a very important thing about their discipleship. He told them it was not enough to *be* disciples; we must go on to *make* disciples (Matthew 28:19). Philip was doing just that on the day he asked Nathanael to come and meet Jesus. He certainly did his part. Philip did not say "Go and see" words of detached indifference; he said, "Come and see", words of supportive compassion. Like Andrew, his fellow-Bethsaidan, "he brought him to Jesus" (1:42). The interview, recorded only in John's gospel, is an illuminating example of personal encounter with Christ. Like the other discipleship stories in this gospel, it will not only explain what happened to Nathanael; it will expound what is important for us.

Nathanael's name only occurs in John 1:44–51, and briefly in this same gospel's fascinating Epilogue in Chapter 21. It is likely that he is the same man as "Bartholomew" in the other gospels. Some of the other disciples are described by more than one name. Jesus called Simon by the name "Peter", meaning "rock", and Levi was also

known as Matthew. The disciple whom Luke twice identifies as "Judas the son of James" (Luke 6:16; Acts 1:13)
is doubtless the one Matthew (10:3) and Mark (3:18)
called "Thaddeus"; one can easily understand why anyone
would prefer a different name from "Judas". We might
say that "Bartholomew" is more the description of the
man's family background than a personal name. It simply
means "son of Tholmai", so he would be likely to have
another name as well.

"Nathanael" was therefore his personal name, and a
very significant name it was too. It meant "God has given"
and every Jewish reader of this gospel would recognize
that by using this name something extremely important
was being declared right at the beginning of Christ's public
ministry. Nathanael stands at the start of the story as a
testimony to the abundant generosity of a God who gives.
In the unpromising context of human cynicism, Nathanael
was taken by a friend to meet Jesus. Before he was scarcely
face to face with Christ he was given a striking indication
of Christ's uniqueness. This unlikely convert was then
enabled, by God's undeserved gift of spiritual insight, publicly to confess the deity of Christ before others. Then he
was given a remarkable vision of the glory of Christ and
the assurance of eternal security.

Over the next few chapters we will look in greater detail
at his initial encounter with the Lord Jesus, for the story
enshrines some timeless truths about our own discipleship.
We begin by noticing that, at their first meeting, the Lord
challenged Nathanael's cynicism.

When Nathanael realized that Philip was trying to persuade him that Israel's Messiah came from a nondescript
place like Nazareth, the shutters immediately crashed
down in his bigoted mind. He knew exactly what he, and

most other people, thought about Nazareth, and there was nothing more to say, except a quick word of sharp dismissal. If we want to introduce people to Jesus, we must recognize that they may well be prejudiced against him from the start. People hear quite a lot about Jesus in our time but most of it is likely to put them off rather than attract them. We too may have to overcome a certain amount of cynicism. People we meet every day have their own reactions to the name "Jesus of Nazareth", the innocent phrase which made Nathanael's hackles rise. Four of them are at once obvious in the late twentieth-century scene; many of our contemporaries are likely to have an image of Christ which is either irrelevant, or innocuous, or controversial or distorted. Each of these needs to be considered if we are to witness effectively to our own generation.

Irrelevant?

When we mention "Jesus of Nazareth", some of them may well think first of the irrelevant Christ of childhood fantasy. They will instinctively recall carefully isolated or grossly embellished stories from their younger days, possibly of occasional contact with Sunday Schools or children's organizations. Naturally, there are magnificent stories from the gospels which are ideal for teaching children, and there is nothing wrong about making the most of such colourful narratives. But they only portray part of the story and, repetitively told to the exclusion of others, they are likely to produce an inaccurate image of the Lord of glory. They may cause Jesus to be dismissed as a childhood irrelevance, along with Father Christmas and other fairy tales, good for easing youngsters into sleep but not for what they were intended – shaking adults out of dangerous inertia.

Especially in the late twentieth century, the contact of many children with churches or Christian organizations is fleeting, to say the least. A recent survey estimates that 86% of all the children in England have no meaningful contact with any church at all.[1] They know little about Jesus. One primary school teacher I know brought immense delight to her "entrants" class by telling them the story of Bethlehem for the very first time; not a single child in the class knew anything about it. A senior teacher in a huge comprehensive school in the West Country told me a similar story about her *leaving* form and showed me a bundle of essays about "The Meaning of Christmas" to prove it. The names of God, Christ, Bethlehem appeared only in two or three and then with no real understanding about the coming of the Son of God. Among children, ignorance or uncertainty are the usual response to the Christmas message, and it is to this generation we are sent.

Trying her utmost to focus interest on centralities when Christmas was approaching, another teacher friend of mine asked her class what happened at Bethlehem. One youngster, eager to reply, called out the name of Jesus, immediately prompting another to shout: "Miss, she's swearing!" In our society, the name of Jesus is most heard on the lips of either careless or ruthless blasphemers. The majority of Britain's children only hear that matchless name in abuse. Their knowledge of Christ as a historical figure may be entirely dependent on what they learn about him in day school. That might well be excellent, but we all know that in many cases it is not. In a pluralistic society like our own, the presentation of Christ in such contexts is in danger of being minimized, marginalized, ignored or distorted.

The distortion may even begin innocently with the story of Christmas, and instead of capturing, even in a simple way, the element of sacrificial love, it can all be grossly fantasized or romanticized beyond recognition. It is a story of bright stars, hospitable stables, lowing cattle, glittering angels, attentive shepherds, adoring oriental visitors. Now all that has elements of truth, if it is also set within the context of the times, and it may not always be easy to do that with children. But if all that is known belongs to the infant school, who will complete the story? If the childlike simplicity of the Bethlehem drama is all that is remembered when the child passes to youth, and then, hearing hardly anything more about Jesus, the child moves on to maturity and adulthood, with only a Christmas fantasy, what portraiture of Christ remains? Who will expound the wonder of the Incarnation, the miracle of God's coming to us uniquely in the person of his Son? Without a messenger to say like Philip, "We have found . . . Come and see" what will be known about the purpose of his coming, about the meaning of his name, about the cost of our salvation, about the fact that right from the beginning, even at Bethlehem, there was either indifference, or pre-occupation, even blatant hostility and cruel rejection?

Even the intentionally bare facts of the biblical story are often crudely coloured, embroidered or falsified. It is all so warm and peaceful, gentle, loving and welcoming. But whoever remembers a matchlessly clean stable or cattle shed, and what serenity could there be with Herod's spies furtively making their whispered enquiries in Bethlehem's streets? If they laid the baby in a manger, his first hours must have been spent in a place which was far from beautiful.

Just after the Second World War, the English missionary, Geoffrey Bull, spent over three years in the prisons and detention centres of the People's Government of China, where he was subjected to their notorious system of brainwashing. At one time, whilst he was being escorted through Sikang, a Tibetan landlord gave the party overnight accommodation in an upstairs room. The missionary had to give some hay to the horses so "clambered down the notched tree trunk to the lower floor, which was given over in the usual manner to stabling". Describing the scene he says:

> Below, it was absolutely pitch black. My boots squelched in the manure and straw on the floor and the fetid smell of the animals was nauseating. I felt my way amongst the mules and horses, expecting to be kicked at any moment. What a place, I thought. Then as I continued to grope my way in the darkness towards the grey it suddenly flashed into my mind. "What's today?" I thought for a moment. In travelling, the days had become a little muddled in my mind. Then it came to me. "It's Christmas Eve". I stood suddenly still in that oriental stable. To think that my Saviour was born in a place like this. To think that he came all the way from heaven to some wretched eastern stable, and what is more, to think that he came for me. How men beautify the cross and crib, as if to hide the fact that at birth we resigned Him to the stench of beasts and at death exposed him to the shame of rogues. God forgive us.[2]

Innocuous?

Others will think of the innocuous Christ of popular entertainment. He may have existed but he belongs to a world so totally unlike our own that his message is meaningless. This Jesus will be the one who appears on the huge wide screen of the local cinema, the Jesus who confronts them from the television drama, the religious celebrity from the ancient world who exercises his ministry of merciful healing more to the background music of expansive, heart-rending orchestral strings rather than bitter jibes, sinister questions and persistent hostility of his forceful opponents. He may be portrayed dramatically as the mythical superman who raises the dead, but in their telling of the story, nothing is likely to be made of Christ's own physical resurrection and nothing of his power to transform the lives of men and women today.

Those notes of confident certainty are missing. Years ago, Dennis Potter's "Son of Man" was watched by millions of television viewers, but it may not have done much to alert them to the Christ of history, the Saviour of sinners, the Conqueror of Death, the Lord of glory, and the Judge of those who deliberately choose to reject him. Throughout that play, Christ was not remotely sure about his Sonship, and its final line confirmed the devastating uncertainty. On the Cross, he does not pray in peaceful trust, "Father, into your hands I commit my spirit" (Luke 23:46), nor do we hear the victorious, one-word *Tetelestai*, the shout of grateful achievement, "It is finished" (John 19:30). It ends with *the* agonizing cry of dereliction, "My God, my God, why have you forsaken *me*" – words that may have found a sad echo in the life of many a lonely viewer ("perhaps even he was not sure") – and who was there to tell them about Easter?

Or, more recently, there has been the sad disillusionment of Jesus as portrayed in the musical "Jesus Christ Superstar". The sense of uncertainty is deliberately conveyed by the haunting question on the lips of the crowd: "Jesus Christ Superstar. Do *you* think you're what they say you are?" It seems that, in that musical, the heart is meant to go out to Judas, the pathetic victim of God's cruel plan:

> For I have been saddled with the murder of you . . .
> I have been dragged through the slime and the mud . . .

> I don't know why he moves me
> He's a man – he's just a man
> He is not a king – he's just the same
> As anyone I know . . .
> God I'll never know why you chose me for your crime.

Discordant?

For some of our contemporaries, however, their cynicism about "Jesus of Nazareth" focuses on the discordant Christ of ecclesiastical controversy. They are understandably bewildered that some of those who take his name seem desperately unsure of his significance, authority, and uniqueness. A leading bishop is certain that Christ was not born of a virgin, that however "alive" he may be in the hearts of minds of modern believers, he was not physically raised from the dead, and that he is not coming back to this earth. No wonder that for some of our neighbours and friends "Jesus of Nazareth" appears to be the Christ of the divisive quarrel, the contentious newspaper article, or of the inconclusive television debate. He is a Jesus to be discussed, analysed, contextualized, demythologized but not *heard and obeyed*.

Disfigured?

Now, more recently, there are people growing up who may only reflect on the Jesus they know through the contemporary film, "The Last Temptation of Christ". Thousands of our contemporaries will only know him through that perverted story; he will be the sadly disfigured Christ of moral indifference. At least one third of the film is taken up with the alleged sexual fantasies of Jesus (with Mary Magdalene) whilst he is on the cross. They are only fantasies, of course, but it is not until the close of the film that one realizes that these are intended as a portrayal of his thoughts and not an aspect of the historical event. Even though at the end of the film they are identified as fantasies, even the notion of a Christ who could indulge in such mental activity at such a sacred moment in his life is totally out of keeping with everything we know about him from the gospels.

The film is naturally offensive to committed Christians but it is also disturbing to anyone who has any regard for historical accuracy. But what of the effect of this film on those who know little about Jesus? For them, far from being spiritually unique, Jesus will be less than morally decent. Earlier generations of film-makers, playwrights and television dramatists were hesitant about portraying him as the Son of God, but they at least tried their utmost to be true to the biblical text. They took the stories in the gospels seriously, and did their best not to stray from the detail in those matchless narratives. Now we have reached the stage when the documentary sources no longer matter, when harmful extraneous embellishments are introduced into the story, and when "Jesus of Nazareth" cannot even be presented as a clean-living human being.

That film's portraiture of Jesus with its perverted fantasies is a sick disgrace. If similar things had been depicted in film of any other religious leader (and we are grateful that, so far, they haven't), there would have been the most enormous protest imaginable and its perpetrators would have been tiraded about offending the sensitivity of other religions, ignoring minority rights, and whatever else. But, sadly, for many of our contemporaries, that historically inaccurate, morally harmful, and spiritually damaging "latest film" portraiture will be the only Christ they know. They will not even have heard about him from their Sunday School days. So, when modern believers venture to say like Philip, "We have found . . . Jesus of Nazareth", those who hear will be astonished that such a humanly unattractive figure should make the slightest appeal to our hearts and minds.

It is sheer folly to assume that the Bible is read seriously anywhere now outside the professing Church and in committed Christian homes. We are in a missionary situation in late-twentieth-century Britain. Moreover, a carefully researched Bible Society survey published a few years ago made the point that almost one third of those people who attend church regularly, seldom or never read the Bible.[3] If we are living in a non-Bible-reading culture, then Christians who want to "make disciples" must use every imaginative means possible to get a gospel into the hands of non-churchgoers. Ministers and preachers have a responsibility to expound the Bible to churchgoers in a way which is so attractive, compelling and relevant, that members of their congregations will go away eager to read the Bible for themselves. However, the actual teaching content in some modern worship services is minimal, and if that continues in those churches in this generation, they will have nobody to preach to in the next. Any form of Christianity which marginalizes the Bible is slowly eroding its own foundation; the frail building will certainly collapse.

In this matchless story of Nathanael's conversion, Philip pointed his friend Nathanael to the Christ of the Scriptures, and modern believers must do the same. For that reason, we are likely to do far more for our contemporaries if we get them to read a gospel than if we lead them into an argument. Across Christian history, thousands of men and women have been brought to personal faith in Jesus simply because they have found him within the pages of the New Testament. Non-churchgoing people have been captivated by Christ by quietly reading the story for themselves. In living and persuasive power he has met them within those brilliant narratives which describe his words and deeds. There is a uniqueness about the Book that describes him as well as about the Lord it portrays. Not all of our contemporaries even know where the story is to be found.

I recall an evening when I sat at a table in a coffee-bar in Torquay talking to an initially hostile youth. His only knowledge of Jesus was what he had retained from his childhood days in school and on his own admission his information was meagre in the extreme. As we quietly talked on, he eventually asked me whether a book had been written about Jesus. Where could he find out the details of the story for himself? At first I thought he was asking for a modern book, some twentieth-century account of Christ's life, but he protested that he didn't want a modern write-up of the story. Surely somebody must have written about Jesus in the first century, and if they hadn't, he wasn't interested. I thought at first he was engaged in playful joking, and said so, but with quiet intense seriousness he assured me that he wasn't joking. He had no idea whatever about where he might look for a written account of the life of our Lord. Even the word "gospel" was new to him. That night he took away in his hand a copy of a New Testament but over the years I have often asked myself how many of his contemporaries are equally unaware of the precise location of this matchless story.

In a spiritually-ignorant society like our own, the modern Nathanaels are not likely to be won unless they can read Christ's story for themselves.

Nicanor Estremera was sent to Princesa Prison in Puerto Rico for attempting to murder a police officer. He was dependent on heroin, cocaine and morphine, and suffering the intense pains of drug withdrawal, with no one to help. He quietly longed for something to take his mind away from himself. One day, in desperation, he called to the man in the next cell, "Luis, do you have something to read?" All Luis had by him was a Bible somebody had given him in hospital. Estremera insisted on having it.

For some reason he started with John's gospel, and couldn't stop reading it. As the days went by, he read on and on, and when he came to 2 Corinthians 5:17 something unexplainable happened. The words seemed to leap at him from the page:

"Therefore, if anyone is in Christ, he is a new creation; the old has gone, the new has come!"

Estremera began to cry uncontrollably. At first he

thought it was the effect of drug withdrawal, but unable to move on the prison floor, he began to be possessed with a sense of deep joy which he had never known before in all his life. He found himself praying to God: "Lord, I have been reading in this book that you have helped others. Will you come and help me too?"

Two months later Nicanor made a public profession of faith at an evangelistic service in the state prison. He told others about his new-found faith and took every opportunity to get his fellow-prisoners together to share his experience of forgiveness, peace and new power. Four years later, he was granted his liberty and, on his release, Christian people were outside the prison, waiting to befriend him. For well over twenty years he has spent most of his time travelling to over twenty countries to tell them of the miracle of a changed life. It all happened because he found Jesus within the pages of God's Word.

If we are to present our neighbours, work-colleagues, fellow-students and friends with the authentic Jesus then we must do everything within our power to encourage them to read a gospel. They are more likely to be confronted by him within the verses of those matchless narratives than by anything that we say to them by way of heated argument. We must always be ready to hear their questions, absorb their criticism, understand their doubts, and meet their difficulties. But we have never been required to have encyclopedic minds which can, in a flash, answer all their enquiries and satisfy every possible objection. When, by what we *are*, they see that, like Philip, we have been "found" by Christ, and once they hear our sensitive, quietly uncompromising word of testimony, "Come and see", all that remains is that we do everything possible to bring them to the place where they might meet with Jesus.

In our case, "Come and see" might be an invitation to a Church Guest Service, a house-group, a Christian Union meeting at school or college, or a local evangelistic event. If unbelievers are to come to Christ they will need that threefold preparation – what they *see* in us (the testimony of a changed life), *read* in the Word (the cost of a changed life), and *hear* from the evangelist (the offer of a changed life). All three of those things are behind Philip's persuasive invitation, "Come and see". Given Nathanael's cynicism, that was all Philip could manage. Nothing more was necessary. Jesus did the rest.

1 Peter Brierley, *"Christian" England: What the English Church Census reveals*, MARC Europe 1991, 60
2 Geoffrey Bull, *When Iron Gates Yield*, Hodder & Stoughton, 1955, 158–59
3 *Attitudes to Bible, God and Church*, British and Foreign Bible Society, 1983

5

SEEING THE BEST IN US

THERE IS an attractive distinctiveness about the call of these disciples in the gospels. In some respect, every meeting is unlike all others. Although there is only one way to the Father, through Christ, there are many different ways in which men and women are brought into the presence of Jesus. When Peter heard Christ's preaching and saw him at work, he was overwhelmed by his guilt: "Go away from me, Lord; I am a sinful man" (Luke 5:8). Matthew the tax collector may well have felt the same. But when Jesus saw Nathanael coming to him, he did not expose his iniquity; he admired his integrity. It was an unusual encounter, and the details are important for an understanding of our own discipleship. We have already seen that Jesus challenged his cynicism. Two further important features emerge in the story: Jesus recognized his qualities and won his allegiance.

Jesus recognized his qualities

As Nathanael approached, Jesus said, "Here is a true Israelite, in whom there is nothing false" (1:47). Jesus knows the worst, but he also sees the best, in us. That is of the utmost importance. At one and the same time, Christ can see us as we are and as we can be. Jesus alone can identify our unique qualities and our best potential. When he looked at Nathanael he could see right through him. He knew all about his cynicism, his superior dismissal of Nazareth as a insignificant town, his snide thoughts when Joseph's name was mentioned. As a devout and well-taught Jew from nearby Cana, he would certainly have heard the unsavoury things which had been said locally about Jesus, Mary and Joseph when the Lord began his ministry, if not earlier. Cruel words and accusations of that kind were soon on the lips of Christ's enemies, "We are not illegitimate children" (John 8:41) – with the deliberately malicious inference, "unlike you"!

If as an ardent, moral, local Jew, Nathanael had ever thought like that, Jesus would certainly have known it at the moment of their first meeting. He knew everything to be known about him. John's gospel makes a special point of emphasizing the unique knowledge of Jesus; it highlights particular events in the ministry of Jesus when that insight was specially manifest. Jesus "knew all men"; nobody was a mystery to him. And nothing was hidden from his gaze: "he knew what was in man" (2:24–25). He knew the deep, inner questions in the mind of Nicodemus before he ever had an opportunity to frame them (3:1–4). He knew the moral decadence of the woman at Sychar's well, even though she tried to hide it all behind a barrage of Samaritan doctrinal sallies (4:16–20). He knew the well-intentioned but dangerous thoughts in the minds of those who by force wanted to make him king (6:15). He knew that the blind man would see later in the day and that "the work of God" would certainly "be displayed in his life" (9:3). He knew that the sickness of his friend, Lazarus, would not "end in death" but would be for the glory of God (11:4). He knew the appalling treachery in the heart of Judas (13:11), when the others had no reason to suspect him and tortured themselves with introspective questions, "Surely not me, Lord?" He knew that, despite the loudest protestations to the contrary, an ostensibly loyal disciple would disown him (13:38).

All that would certainly emerge during the ministry of Christ but, on the day Philip said "Come and see", Nathanael had no reason to believe that Jesus had such unique insight into human nature, and could read the thoughts in the mind of this studious, good-living man from Cana. He was amazed when, quietly and confidently, Jesus introduced him, a "total stranger", to those who were standing by. Nathanael was astonished. It was natural to express his bewilderment: "How do you know me?" What did it all mean when Jesus spoke of him as an "Israelite . . . in whom there is nothing false" (1:47)?

Jesus knew how much Nathanael loved the Old Testament Scriptures, and there are clear indications from his conversation here that when he described Nathanael in those terms he was making a deliberate contrast between this Israelite and the original Israelite, Jacob, the one who was named "Israel" first of all. Christ had plumbed the depths of Nathanael's heart and knew, as no one else, the genuineness and sincerity of the man. Unlike scheming, deceitful Jacob in the Old Testament, here was a man who was true, open and honest, through and through. He may have been critical of Jesus but at least he was real. He did not say one thing when in reality he was utterly different. In that sense, he stood head and shoulders above many of his religious superiors, the Pharisees of his day. They were like newly white-washed tombs on the outside, parading their religious observances and ostentatious good works when, all the time, their secret lives were corrupt with unclean thoughts, greedy ambitions, petty jealousies, and self-indulgent habits (Matthew 23:25–28).

There was nothing of that in Nathanael. Like the Pharisees, poor Jacob had been a hypocrite if anybody had. That ugly word, hypocrite, belongs to the language of Greek drama; it describes someone who wears a mask and plays a part. Jacob was as deceptive as it was possible to be. He deliberately deceived his old father, leading the frail, sightless man to believe that he was his elder brother (Genesis 27:1–40). When the ruse is exposed, the grief-stricken father, Isaac, tells his other son "Your brother came *deceitfully* and took your blessing" (Genesis 27:35). In the Greek version of the Old Testament, the Septuagint, the word is the same as that used by Jesus in the Nathanael story. It sharply points the contrast. There was no *deceit* in Nathanael. This potential disciple was made of different stuff, and Jesus was glad of it.

In the Jacob story, when the greedy cheat's misrepresentation was exposed, he fled from home and, pursued by his angry brother, had an encounter with God by means of an unforgettable dream. Centuries later, on that day Nathanael first met Jesus, the Lord reminded him of that story of Jacob's flight by using some vivid descriptive words lifted straight from the story of the patriarch. When Jesus saw Nathanael he knew that, for all his undoubted faults, there was no Jacob-like duplicity in him. Jesus identified Nathanael's choice qualities as well as his inevitable sins.

We must remember this when we come to think of our discipleship. Jesus knew that there were useful gifts and attractive features about his personality, and he sees the same in us. Of course, we are all sinners, but when we speak sometimes of "total depravity" we are saying that sin is total in its extent. We mean that it has invaded *all* our lives and has sadly affected *every* part of us, but it does not mean that we are all totally incapable of doing anything at all that is good and helpful. Far from it. Total depravity means that we can never by our good works do anything to win the favour of a righteous God but it does not mean that we are totally incapable of kindness, sincerity, good behaviour and high ideals. It means that at some point or other, sin spoils things, and that our highest and best things cannot make us right with God. Jesus knew that to be as true of Nathanael as anybody else, but he still wanted to identify the best in him and not just expose the worst in him.

Jesus sees the best in us too. When he saw Martin Luther in the sixteenth century, he knew how genuinely penitent and remorseful he was, and he knew that such a sensitive spirit and such a fine, alert mind could begin to lead a reformation. When he drew John Bunyan to himself in the following century, he knew that although the Bedfordshire metal-worker was as poorly-educated as it was possible to be, there were under the surface natural literary gifts which, in persecution and enforced seclusion, would be developed to bring blessing to millions over the succeeding centuries. When in the eighteenth century, he led John Wesley to that meeting in Aldersgate Street, he did not only look at the Anglican priest's earlier reliance on good works, or his occasional spiritual superiority, or his failures in Georgia, but at the man's better qualities and unbelievably rich potential. He could see him not as the burdened introvert who went to that May-evening meeting, but as an imaginative evangelist who, having experienced that dejection, would ride the length and breadth of the land preaching the good news of Christ. Jesus saw him not just as he was but as he could be, a tireless traveller, riding over 200,000 miles, preaching over 40,000 sermons, a strenuous campaign which lasted over fifty years.

In that same century, Jesus saw the uncouth captain of a slave-trading ship, but looked beyond his blasphemy, moral depravity and corruption to what John Newton could and would be, once given the grace to turn from his sins. Christ saw the astonishing gifts as well as the blatant degradation, the hidden virtues beneath the evident vice. Jesus could see Newton as he was going to be, "a true Israelite, in whom there is nothing false". He saw the faithful evangelical preacher, the compassionate pastor, the helpful letter-writer, the gifted hymnist encouraging others to trust in God's "amazing grace".

Disciples need to be reminded that Christ has not come into the world to deprive us of anything but things which destroy us. He has come not to subtract, but to add to our life in generous abundance. It is the devil's ploy to point out the things we may have to lose if we come to the Saviour. But it is the enemy who is the robber, as Jesus made clear to his men during his talks with them: "The thief comes only to steal and kill and destroy; I have come that they may have life, and have it to the full" (John 10:10).

Following Jesus as Nathanael did means that, from the start, you are in the company of one who not only sees you as you are, but as you can be. Knowing our true potential, he beckons us on to better things. What he did for Nathanael, he did for the others. He saw beyond Peter's sins to Peter's success: "from now on you will catch men"

(Luke 5:10). He saw beyond the tax-collector's suspect accountancy to Matthew's gifted literacy, to the superb gospel which would one day bear his name. He does the same with us, looks far beyond our immediate faults and perceptible failings to the people he can make us, by his grace alone. True discipleship is not simply abandoning the things that are wrong in our lives, just as Matthew left his dishonest occupation; it is responding to the call of one who sees the best in us, and is determined to release those concealed gifts and realize that enormous potential.

Jesus won his allegiance

When Nathanael asked Jesus, "How do you know me?" the words literally mean "Where do you know me from?" It's rather as we, puzzled about someone's identity, might say, "Sorry, but where have we met before?" Jesus told him in effect that, though Nathanael had known nothing about it, he had met with him when he was at the place of quiet prayer and spiritual meditation. The Hebrew people used that phrase "under the fig tree" to describe the place of domestic privacy and personal intimacy (Isaiah 36:16; Micah 4:4; Zechariah 3:10). What stunned Nathanael that day was not simply that Jesus had looked deeply into his present inner life, but that Christ knew about his past, well before the moment when Philip mentioned "Jesus of Nazareth". That truth blew Nathanael's mind. A sensitive preacher from those Galilean villages might well hazard a guess about the inmost thoughts of a devout student of the Hebrew Law, a genuine seeker after God with a local reputation for attractive righteousness. But how could any human being profess to know all there was to be known about another man's past, and to have looked deeply into the heart of Nathanael long before his friend had told him of Christ? Those were the words which drove Nathanael to a radical change of mind about Jesus: "I saw you while you were still under the fig tree before Philip called you" (1:48). However was such a thing possible, unless Jesus was all he claimed to be?

It was that which brought Nathanael to total surrender. Only God can know us fully and completely (Psalm 139; Hebrews 4:13). Here was somebody who was not gently guessing at a neighbour's spirituality. Jesus was telling him in the plainest possible terms that he was God's Son, able not only to look deeply into Nathanael's mind but to look backwards and forwards along the corridor of time and see where Nathanael was at, what he was doing, what he might do, would do, could do, if changed and redeemed. Here was one who had come to him not only as the revealer of Nathanael but as the unique reflection and perfect revealer of God. That truth brought Nathanael to personal faith in Jesus, and to his unashamed public acknowledgment of Christ as his Revealer, God and King. But that confession and what follows is a massive theme in itself, and we must turn to it in our next chapter.

6

LISTENING IN

It was an overwhelming moment for Nathanael when he realized that Jesus knew everything about him. Is it possible that the Lord knew not only where he had been sitting ("under the fig tree") but even what he had been reading? Christ's description of him by the name of "Israelite", his reference to "no guile", and especially his direct quotation from Jacob's ladder-dream (Genesis 28:12) suggest the possibility that, at the very moment his friend Philip came to share his exciting discovery about Jesus as the fulfiller of Scripture, Nathanael may have been meditating on the story of Jacob. At that time he may have been reading about Jacob's guile, the giving at Bethel of the patriarch's new name "Israel" (Genesis 35:6–10) and the account of God's earlier meeting with him at the same place (Genesis 28:12). Jesus turns to address the small group gathered around Nathanael: "I say to you *all*, you shall see heaven open"; the "you" there is plural, not singular as if to Nathanael alone. Heaven is open not only to Jacob at Bethel, and not solely for Nathanael, here and now. Jacob had made his personal response to the revelation of God:

"This is the gate of heaven", and now Nathanael was about to make his, later to be followed by millions more.

The thought that Christ was not only portrayed in the Scripture centuries earlier but could direct the mind of a contemporary Bible-reader from the page to his Person, made Nathanael realize that he was in the presence of someone unique. Here was no mere travelling preacher, local wonder-worker, or yet another Galilean political revolutionary. What ancient Scripture and contemporary disciples like Andrew and Philip were saying about him was gloriously true, and the convinced Nathanael makes his personal response to the revelation just as, centuries before, young Jacob had made his. In the closing verses of this narrative (John 1:49–51), it is not only Nathanael who is enabled to "Come and see" (1:46); we too are brought to the place where we are also encouraged to do it ourselves. What is plain for us all to see from the climax of this memorable narrative is what Jesus does for Nathanael is the "gift of God" to all his disciples in every generation: Jesus inspires every believer's personal and public confession.

Within a short space of time Nathanael is changed from a casual enquirer to an unashamed believer, from sarcastic dismissal to deep conviction. The narrative leads us through five clear stages of this new disciple's spiritual experience. We see his progress, first, from detached cynicism ("Nazareth...") to puzzled curiosity (willingly responding to Philip's "Come and see"), then on to sincere enquiry ("How do you know me?"), and from there to convinced allegiance ("You are ... you are"), and finally to public affirmation.

It is this triple acclamation of Jesus as Nathanael's Teacher, God's Son and Israel's King that is as important for an understanding of our own discipleship as well as an insight into his. We must look now at the first of these three important aspects of his confession – Nathanael's Teacher.

Jesus is first acknowledged as Nathanael's Teacher: "Rabbi", says the newly convinced disciple. The title is to recur throughout this gospel (4:31; 6:25; 9:2; 11:8) and, right from the start, we are not left to guess at the meaning of that significant form of address. This opening chapter in John's gospel informs us that "Rabbi" means "Teacher" (1:38), and here Nathanael begins by telling Jesus that, like Andrew and Philip, he too wants to become a learner. That is surely the first step for every disciple – to be willing to hear and do what Jesus says. It is the disciple's necessary response to the call to obedience.

The next person to take the title of "Rabbi" on his lips in this gospel is Nicodemus, another Jew who knows the Scripture well. He begins his conversation with Christ by affirming that he and a number of his contemporaries believe that Jesus is "a teacher who has come from God" (3:2). But, though Nicodemus recognizes Jesus as an outstanding "teacher" in Israel, there are a number of things he has yet to learn (3:10), including the crucial message of the "new birth". Once again, like Nathanael, Nicodemus is taken back to the pages of the Old Testament, once more to the Pentateuch. Nathanael had been sensitively directed to the experience of Jacob; now Nicodemus is reminded of the message of Moses (3:14). As with Nathanael, it is still the message of "heaven", and of the Son of Man, coming to this earth as the promised Saviour (3:13) and leaving this world as the eternal Victor, the one who, like the serpent in the desert (Numbers 21:4–9) was "lifted up" on the Cross so that the mortal wounds of human sin might be healed for ever.

Yet, however carefully Nicodemus had read that narrative in the writings of Moses, he would not have grasped its true and deeper meaning unless Christ had been his teacher that night he went to see Jesus privately (3:1). The story of the bronze replica of that snake in the wilderness would have stayed as a dramatic tale of what happened to Moses rather than of what might happen to him. Nicodemus came to see that he too could be healed by what that story typified. But, well-taught as he was in the Jewish Scripture, how could he see the truth about "what Moses wrote about in the Law" (1:45) unless, like Nathanael, he had an interpreter?

The night Jesus talked with Nicodemus, there were three times when he began a fresh sentence with a penetrating phrase he had used earlier in his conversation with Nathanael – "I tell you the truth" (3:3, 5, 11; 1:51). Literally, the words read, "Amen, Amen I say to you". It was quite common for a rabbi to use that solemn word "Amen" to drive a point home with special strength, but he usually put the word at the end of his sentence, not at its beginning, and he never repeated it as Jesus did. This double-amen is found only in "John"; in the other gospels Jesus begins an important statement by saying, "Amen, I say to you", but in this gospel the repeated word is found twenty-five times. It must be there for special emphasis. The world's greatest communicator is making a point with great forcefulness, urgency and relevance. It is a word of a unique teacher and it must be heard, treasured and obeyed.

Teaching is extremely important in "John". The first introduction of Jesus in this gospel is as "the Word" (1:1).

The Father has something of outstanding importance to say to us in Jesus, the Word of God. It is an eternal Word (1:1) from one who has always been with God, a creative Word which brought the universe into being (1:3), an illuminating Word, conveying for ever the love and life of the Father, a word "full of grace and truth" (1:14, 17), an authoritative Word for, as John the Baptist perceived, "the one whom God has sent speaks the words of God, for God gives the Spirit (to him) without limit" (3:34). In other words, we are being told right at the beginning of "John" that God's word to us in Christ is unique. Moreover, the emphasis on the necessity of good teaching is constantly underlined in John's later chapters. In those chapters, 14 to 16, which contain the "Upper Room Discourse", Jesus repeatedly emphasizes the importance of his message by saying to his disciples, "All this I have told you so that . . ." (15:11; 16:1, 4, 6, 25, 33).

Like Nathanael and Nicodemus and all his followers, we too need a Teacher. If we are to respond meaningfully to the call to discipleship, our minds must also be informed as theirs were when they first met with Jesus. There are things we must grasp as "learners", and that will not happen automatically. We must find time for it. How is it to be achieved in our frequently overcrowded lives? Christ wants to be our Teacher privately, corporately and publicly.

Listen privately

First, we must meet with our Teacher privately. Every Christian needs to find some time in every day for personal Bible reading and prayer. There can be no easy substitute for the regular discipline of a daily "Quiet Time", or whatever we may like to call it. Jesus told his disciples that they were to meet with God in that way (Matthew 6:6) and not make a public show of our spirituality as the Pharisees did in his day. Jesus not only taught the importance of a personal devotional life; he exemplified it by getting up early in the morning to spend time with God. The more busy he became, the more important it was for him to escape from the public place to enter the secret place of communion with God (Mark 1: 35; Matthew 14:23; Luke 5:16) so that he could surrender himself afresh to his Father at the beginning of each new day.

It is clear from the example of Jesus that there are three vital ingredients for this pattern of practical, daily spirituality – discipline, quietness, and submission. But these are not common commodities in our world. Discipline is unfashionable, quietness is rare, and submission is challenged. Let's look at each of them.

We have to recognize that, in the contemporary scene, discipline is unfashionable. In today's world, the emphasis is on spontaneity, freedom, and emotional subjectivity. You only do things if you feel like doing them, not because they *must* be done. It is part of the culture of late-twentieth-century society, but it has disastrous effects when it is adopted, often imperceptibly, as a pattern for Christian living. Jesus lived a disciplined life, and his disciples cannot hope to follow him effectively without one.

If we are to have a Quiet Time in each day, it will be necessary to plan for it, and think carefully about when the best time might be in our particular case. Life is not stereotyped for us as believers. For some people, the best time undoubtedly is before doing anything else in the morning. For others, the moment the alarm-clock goes off is not the best time. Our work may demand an exceptionally early start and we may find that a later time suits us best. Many people who have to commute to work find it helpful to give themselves to quiet prayer and Bible reading during their morning train journey. Actually, it can be quite encouraging to see the number of people on a morning train who study God's Word on their way to work. Others deliberately catch an earlier train so that they can go into a city church on their way to the office or shop, and spend fifteen or twenty minutes there quietly with God, reading his Word, listening to his voice, seeking his strength for the service and opportunities of the day. The housewife may well find that the best time is when the children are off to school; other people may need to look out for a different kind of "slot" in the day. But unless we plan for it, then it is not likely to happen, and planning it and keeping to our appointment with God demands discipline, but that is surely an essential aspect of discipleship.

Another factor about the contemporary scene which militates against the Quiet Time is that quietness is rare. We live in an extremely noisy world. Many of our neighbours cannot cope with stillness and silence; in such a world it is not easy to be quiet. People travel with their "Walkman" transistors or tape-players booming in their ears; in many homes televisions or radios are left on most of the day. The background of incessant noise appears to be an essential ingredient in the late-twentieth-century world. But Christian believers know that, like Jesus, they must find some opportunity to retreat or escape from all that for at least a few minutes in each day, so that, above the noise of the everyday contemporary life, the Lord can quietly speak to them through his ever-relevant Word.

A further aspect of contemporary thought which creates subconscious difficulties for practical Christian spirituality is that, in our modern culture, submission is challenged. "Authority" is not an acceptable notion in the modern scene. People are slow to recognize objective standards or values which in any way run counter to their own preconceived ideas or thought patterns. Ours is an age much like that which is described in the Book of Judges: "everyone did as he saw fit" (17:6; 21: 25). Many of our contemporaries are offended by the notion that God, or anybody else, can dictate how we should behave. The thought that we should surrender our lives to him and obey what he says is anathema to the modern mind. Ethical standards are all right as long as they do not interfere with what we want to do. They might well serve as appropriate norms for general behaviour but they are certainly not to be enforced. This is the era of "situation ethics"; this or that pattern of moral conduct needs to be accommodated to their particular situation. There are no inflexible moral principles, it is maintained, neither given by God or religion, tradition or society.

"Authority" is regarded as an inhibiting concept; men and women must be free. But Jewish believers like Philip and Nathanael would have been astonished by such reasoning. Their word for Law, "Torah" meant "a path to walk on", a "particular direction", a safe route to keep us free from harm. They fervently believed that God defined our paths for life in his Law, knowing that there are menacing perils if those laws were disobeyed. The Ten Commandments might sound restrictive to an untutored ear but they mark out a safe and reliable pathway for our society as well as in Moses' day. No community can be happy if people are made to work like slaves day in and day out, without assured periods of rest. Who can be happy in a society where elderly people are despised, ignored or neglected? Where can anybody feel "safe" within a community if there is no respect whatever for life, or truth, or the law of property? Are families made happier by adultery? Are covetous people nice to know? Yet these are the issues which are firmly dealt with by the Ten Commandments, and the Lord God knows that, when they are dismissed, people are unhappy.

For a couple of summer holidays I have enjoyed walking quite long stretches of the Pembrokeshire Coast Path with my son. We were regularly confronted with notices like this: "It is dangerous to stray from the path", and at other places "Cliffs kill". But, how ridiculously restrictive, someone might say. Yet those warning signs are not designed to limit my freedom but secure it, so that I might continue to live. That is why God's word came so clearly through Moses, "Follow them so that you may live" (Deuteronomy 4:1; 32:47). God's laws, like my frequent coastal path warnings, have been provided for my protection. If I ignore the warnings, I may plunge to my death. Every year some person or other, intent on enjoying their "freedom", chooses to dismiss the cautionary notices and dies by falling from the coastal paths. What use is "freedom" to them?

Christ confronts us with his own teaching, and disciples listen to what he has to say. They know that he wants us to enjoy life and "have it to the full" (10:10). He came specially into the world to secure that blessing for us, and if he warns us against something, we can be sure that, however attractive it may appear, such things are dangerous and destructive. He is the "way and the truth and the life" (14:6), and has marked out in his own person, life and teaching the best path for us to follow.

Once we have found the right time and the quiet place, we obviously need some kind of method so that we can get the very best out of our daily time of communion with God. Some systematic pattern of Bible study is an excellent thing. Daily Bible-reading notes such as those published by Scripture Union, or other similar notes, are an immense help in discovering for ourselves the rich truths of God's Word. But we also need to have a personal notebook handy so that we do not simply read the printed comments of a daily Bible-reading note, but also write down perhaps *one thing* which the Lord is saying to us through that particular passage of Scripture we have studied that day.

Some Christians have found it helpful in these times to keep a spiritual journal so that they can record the precise things which the Lord has said to them, and how they are to be applied to their own lives. They have used the journal to note down special items for prayer, specific answers to prayer and, on occasions, spiritual transactions with God which they wished to register in his presence.

Studying corporately

Secondly, we may meet with our Teacher corporately. We are likely to learn a great deal about the Christian life if we meet regularly for Bible study with other believers. Jesus called twelve men to be alongside him in the work and he knew only too well that, in the years ahead, they would be able to encourage each other. The disciples were not only learners; they were partners. In this gospel of John, some of them, like Andrew and Philip, seemed to be specially close to one another. Such men would be partners in learning as well as colleagues in service. They had things they wanted to discover about Christ together.

We would all be greatly enriched by the teaching ministry of the Lord Jesus if we were able to find definite opportunities to meet with him in the presence of a group of fellow-believers. Many people do that frequently through church or home Bible study groups, Christian Union meetings at school, college or work, and in other contexts. When we study a passage alongside other Christians, new insights may be given to us which we might not have discovered in quite the same way on our own. Each of us can become rather tightly locked into familiar thought-patterns. When we turn to a well-known passage of Scripture on our own, it may well say much the same kind of thing as it did when last we read it. But, in the company of other believers new insights may be given to us, and to them through us as well.

The Lord Jesus was certainly not a "loner". Even the Son of God valued a team about him, and appreciated the physical support, prayerful love and practical help that the group of disciples could bring. If the Saviour refused to "go it alone", then surely it would be fatal for us to do so. Jesus knew that when he had ascended to heaven, the promised Holy Spirit would exercise a wide-ranging teaching-ministry among his followers. In the course of that ministry, the Spirit would remind the disciples of things which Jesus had said to them, but sayings which, in the pressure of busy lives, had receded from the forefront of their thinking. He would reveal new things, or state familiar truths in new forms, to inspired and gifted men like Paul, Peter, John, James, Jude, and their colleagues. That truth would be eagerly received and greatly treasured within the early Christian communities, and across the years these early Christian people would have so much to learn from what the Spirit was saying through their fellow-believers.

Unlike them, we are immeasurably blessed by having, easily to hand, God's unique Word in both Old and New Testaments, and we are certainly not looking for totally new and different revelations of his mind and will. If we receive either personally or in a group, some "message" or "vision" of God's will and purpose for us, we will all want to check that against what is clearly taught in Scripture, for that book is God's distinctive way of revealing his truth to us. Everything else must be totally subservient to the message of the Bible; that is God's unique, distinctive, authoritative and changeless Word, and our submission must be to that Word alone.

But that does not mean that we are meant to discern its truth on our own. So much of the Bible's message may be waiting for us to appreciate and appropriate it, simply because we have not yet studied it as carefully as we might with other believers, disciples who are just as concerned as ourselves to be Christ's attentive and obedient learners in today's world.

Learning publicly

Thirdly, we can listen to our Teacher publicly. Right down from biblical times, the public exposition of God's Word is a unique means he is pleased to use in communicating his truth to us. Jesus made it his custom (Luke 4:16) every Sabbath day to go to the local synagogue to listen to the public reading and interpretation of the Old Testament.

When he met with his disciples he made a special point of teaching them the truths of God's Word (Luke 24:45) and he also took every possible opportunity to communicate by preaching to a wider audience. John's gospel, like the others, records a number of occasions when he taught in the Jerusalem Temple, local synagogues and in other public places (6:59; 7:14, 28; 8:2, 20).

Jesus continues to communicate his truth through faithful and relevant Christian preaching. Luke makes it clear that the early Christian people regularly listened to the public exposition of Scripture, and throughout the Acts of the Apostles we are constantly finding ourselves in some congregation or other listening to the careful explanation and application of what God is saying through his Word (1:15–22; 2:14–41; 3:11–26; 6:15 – 7:53; 13:14–43; 17:16–34; 20:17–38).

The exposition of their Bible (the Old Testament) was extremely important to these people, and it must be for us as well if we are to grow and develop in the Christian life. Time and again, in the lives of millions of people, God has been pleased to speak to them directly through the clear and persuasive preaching of biblical truth. Every Christian needs to be in a church where that kind of relevant expository ministry is a central feature in Sunday worship and possibly at other times in the week as well.

Throughout history, men and women have heard the clear word of Jesus come to them through the faithful teaching of a Christian preacher. Such ministers of God's Word have an immense responsibility. Their part is to be loyal to the biblical text, eager to relate it to life in today's world, and long to present the message in an interesting and attractive form. With such a fascinating book as the Bible, and such an exciting message to share, the preacher's greatest dread is to be boring. To do it well, expository teaching demands consistently careful, thorough and dedicated work on the part of the preacher. But the congregation have a vital part to play in the enterprise as well. They will want to pray regularly for their minister or Christian leader as he prepares; they also need to ask the Lord for attentiveness to the Word as it is expounded, obedience to what God may be saying to them through it, and a willingness to share it with others.

Two things will be uppermost in the minds of true disciples whenever they listen to Christ their Teacher through the public exposition of Scripture – an eagerness to store his truth and share it.

First, we must never judge the preaching of God's Word by the superficial test of its *immediate* relevance. After all, in any congregation, people are bound to be there with a wide variety of differing needs. There will obviously be times when the message given by the expositor will come to us forcefully with striking and direct appeal; it is something that we specially needed at that particular moment of time, and it seemed as if the preacher was speaking to us alone.

But it cannot always be like that, and it is not right that it should. After all, on some occasions the Lord may be giving us a truth which we are meant to store carefully in our minds, to prepare or equip us for some future experience. God's truth is meant to build us up and make us into mature Christians, people whose faith is firmly built on a solid and reliable biblical foundation. To change the imagery, we must not allow the seed of God's Word to be tossed away as "irrelevant" or "not applicable to my present circumstances". The day may come when it could not possibly be more relevant. A mature believer knows that, and hides God's Word in the heart so that it can be recalled, given time to grow and produce fruit.

Secondly, we must always remember when we hear the public exposition of Scripture that the Word has not simply been given for ourselves alone. Possibly the Lord is communicating that particular truth through the preacher that day so that we can pass it on to someone else. If we listen carefully, the regular and systematic exposition of Scripture will do more than anything else to equip us with a Christian "mind" on many of the big issues in life. It will not simply help us to grow as believers; it will give us the resources we need to help other people with their problems and difficulties. So, whenever we listen to Christian preaching, let's remember that the message is not simply for "now", nor is it only for "us"; we must store it and share it.

7

AFFIRMING OUR LOYALTY

WE HAVE SEEN that Nathanael responded to Christ by, first of all, acknowledging his need of Jesus as his Teacher. We must do that too, and recognize that he speaks to us privately in our own daily Quiet Time, corporately through group Bible Study, and publicly through the faithful exposition of Scripture. Nathanael then went on to declare his allegiance to Jesus as God's Son and Israel's King.

God's Son

"Rabbi (Teacher)", says Nathanael, "you are the Son of God" (1:49). Openly and unequivocally, this new disciple acknowledged Christ's unique deity. Nathanael's response to Jesus makes it clear that though Christ is our essential Teacher and Revealer of truth he is something far more than that. He is the matchless, incomparable Son of God. The Teacher is to be obeyed, but the Son is to be worshipped. By introducing in the opening paragraphs this public confession by Nathanael, the author of this gospel has announced one of his great central themes: the adoration of God's Son. John later tells us that he has written his gospel for that very purpose, to bring others, as well as Nathanael, to personal acknowledgment of the deity of Christ, "that you may believe that Jesus is the Christ, the Son of God" (20:31).

This gospel begins with a public confession of Christ's deity from the mouth of a doubter, Nathanael: "Nazareth! Can anything good come from there?" It also ends with an acknowledgment of Christ's Sonship on the lips of a more surprising sceptic, Thomas: "My Lord and my God" (20:28). That theme of the uniqueness of God's Son is a constantly reiterated theme in "John". It forms part of the magnificent Prologue (1:14, 18) which "sets the stage" for later teaching. From the start, John the Baptist testifies to the truth of that key doctrine (1:34). In this gospel the Father gives His Son (3:16), sends him (3:17), loves him (3:35; 5:20), uses him (5:19), and glorifies him (13:32). In this gospel Jesus declares himself to be God's Son (10:29–30, 36), others also testify to that truth (11:27) and, as we have seen, it is hoped that we too will make the same confession (20:31).

With this adoring confession we have reached the heart of Christian truth. Nobody can possibly be a Christian in the New Testament definition of that term without acknowledging Christ's deity. Yet this is the very point of departure for those who want to restrict their portraiture of Jesus to the fascinating teacher, or the outstanding example, or the inspiring leader. Many of the vast number of new emerging religions will find a place for Jesus somewhere in their system, but they will not confess his deity. Jehovah's Witnesses will argue with confidence on our doorsteps about a wide range of their bizarre ideas, but they will balk at any suggestion that Jesus is God's only Son. In their view he is only "a" son of God, as others may be. New religions, cults and sects are mushrooming year by year at an astonishing rate. There is the Church of Scientology, for example, with its aim of steering the individual "out of the problems and seeming restrictions of everyday life, to a point where he can gain higher levels of spiritual freedom"[1] but, in their teaching, it can all be achieved without Christ, Son of God.

Many of the new religions make their appeal to the divine presence within every one of us. But the teaching of Scripture is that by nature we are not "divine"; although made initially in the image of God and able to respond to him, by nature we are "lost" people, and in order to know God personally, we need to be found by him. However, one of the many new sects, "Eckenkar", is "based upon individual experience with the ECK (Spirit) – that divine essence within each of us".[2]

The increasingly fashionable "New Age" teaching is a bizarre mixture of religious and philosophical ideas, and that also maintains that each person is God. In a recent study of new religious movements, Dr Eileen Barker has observed that most of the people "connected with New Age would see themselves as seekers who are exploring new and exciting frontiers". Some of them maintain a syncretistic approach to other faiths and ally themselves with several other religious groups; others have totally rejected traditional religious and philosophical concepts, regarding them as "bankrupt".[3] The human transformation which "New Age" teachers present is that individual men and women need to actualize their divine nature, and become the God they are. This can be achieved through various techniques such as yoga, chanting, and hypnosis.

For some "New Age" people, their ideas may include some concepts and values which are part of the Christian message but there is no place in any of their teaching for any acknowledgment of Jesus as *the* Son of God.

As in this gospel we are allowed to overhear Nathanael's confession of Christ's deity, we are surely meant to recognize the distinctiveness of Christianity, even in an age of religious pluralism. The New Testament message of the uniqueness of Christ is bound to be an offence to people who have chosen to give their allegiance to other religions. But this gospel, possibly with greater definiteness than any other, tells us with unmistakable clarity that "No-one comes to the Father" except through Jesus, God's only Son (14:6).

What then is a modern Christian to do about people who live all around us yet who own a different religion altogether? What about our Muslim, Buddhist, and Hindu neighbours? Are they pursuing authentic and alternative ways to the one God, or are they misled in their teaching? Surrounded as they were with substitute salvations, the early Christian people were unequivocal in their answers to that kind of question. Irritating as it may have been to their contemporaries, they shared their conviction with unshakable certainty: "Salvation is found in no-one else, for there is no other name under heaven given to men by which we must be saved" (Acts 4:12). That uncompromising teaching has never been rescinded. In a pluralistic age, it assuredly provides us with the certainty we need. But it does not give us the authority to be arrogantly or coldly dismissive towards people whose greatly treasured faith is in other world religions. How then are we to relate to the many thousands of people in our own Western culture who do not subscribe to our conviction that Jesus is God's unique Son? There are six basic principles. We need to learn, listen, serve, share, pray and love.

First, we have a Christian responsibility to *learn*. We cannot hope to have good things to share with people of other faiths if we do not know our own. They have strong convictions, and they are fully entitled to them. However firmly we hold our own beliefs, we must always be grateful for our religious freedom, which means essentially that other people can hold their views with equal tenacity and with the same liberty to share those views as we enjoy. But the trouble is that many Christians do not know their faith really well. The presence of so many people now in Western society with a faith that we once associated with distant lands, is surely a challenge to every believer to "know the certainty of the things" we "have been taught" (Luke 1:4). The gospel of John has so much to say about "the truth" that is ours in Christ, but we must *know* it well if we want to share it effectively.

Secondly, we must *listen* to what our non-Christian neighbours have to say about their faith. We have no right to declare our belief in Christ unless we have taken the time to hear what they have to tell us about the convictions that are dear to them. Even if we do not personally know people who confess an allegiance to other world religions, we ought to take the time and trouble to read about their views so that we are the better informed should opportunities come our way for personal witness. Well-informed and inexpensive paperbacks are available on the major non-Christian religions with useful suggestions as to how we may better understand the beliefs of our neighbours in this global village. Some of us live in cities, towns or villages where at present we are unlikely to meet a committed Muslim or a devout Buddhist, but in our society that situation is not likely to continue for long. In any case, it does not mean that even for the present we are free to ignore this important subject of the relationship between Christianity and other world religions. The pluralistic context of our time has caused many of our contemporaries to shelter behind the notion that "all religions are equal" and thus avoid the direct confrontation they might otherwise meet in a distinctive New Testament message. For their sakes, as well as others, we ought to know the basic tenets of other faiths and what God's Word has to say about some of those ideas.

Thirdly, we must *serve*. Our desire to honour Christ as his disciples will surely drive us out in compassionate service to others, and we will not want to restrict that service solely to people who subscribe to our distinctive Christian teaching. There will be opportunities within local communities to do things for other people whether they have another faith or no faith. In some localities where there are people who subscribe to other religious views, there may be opportunities for service through language experience groups, friendship centres, playgroups, coffee mornings, luncheon clubs, where we can meet with non-Christian people and endeavour to help them in every way within our power. Meals can be delivered to sick or elderly neighbours whatever their religion, letters can be written, shopping done, gardens dug for the elderly, kindness shown, and all in the name of Christ.

Fourthly, we can *share* our faith with people of other religions or none. Given the right opportunity, the message of Christ, the only Saviour, can be sensitively and attractively presented and our neighbours who profess to believe in other religions may well be glad to know more about him. In this gospel of John, Christ's truth is shared not only with devout Jewish people but with their despised neighbours, the Samaritans (4:7–26). Jesus told his disciples that a harvest of Samaritan souls was waiting to be reaped at the very moment when they kept on urging him to eat his meal. He had better things to do just then. "Open your eyes and look at the fields. They are ripe for harvest. Even now the reaper draws his wages, even now he harvests the crop for eternal life" (4:35–36). The Samaritan villagers had heard the testimony of the newly-liberated woman and came to hear for themselves the truth of Christ (4:39–43). And the truth they eagerly grasped that day was "that this man really is the Saviour of the world" (4:42), not just the Saviour of Jews but of their religiously outcast Samaritan neighbours also.

Moreover, it is this same gospel of John which tells us about Greeks who came to the Passover festival and wanted to see Jesus (12:20), and this great missionary gospel has assured its readers throughout the centuries that "God so loved *the world* that he gave his only begotten Son, that *whoever* believes in him shall not perish but have eternal life" (3:16). It is the Good Shepherd distinctively portrayed in this same gospel who tells his Jewish followers that he has "other sheep that are not of this sheep pen" and that he "must bring them also. They too will listen to my voice, and there shall be one flock and one shepherd" (10:16).

The memorable Passion narrative in this gospel uses the opportunity to convey, even in the last moments of Christ's earthly life, the notes of universal missionary appeal. The declaration of his kingship above the Cross announced its message in the three major tongues of the first-century world – Hebrew (Aramaic), Latin and Greek – the languages of religion, politics, and philosophy. It is as if in his gospel John is grasping a final opportunity to say once again that this Saviour died for all men and women, the wide world over, and his disciples have the privilege of sharing that good news with others. In his Easter message, Christ is the great Missionary Exemplar: "As the Father has sent me, I am sending you" (20:21).

Fifthly, we must *pray* for our non-Christian neighbours and for people of other religions within our culture as well as in other parts of the world. It is important for us to put the names of Jewish friends or Muslim neighbours or Hindu shop assistants or Rastafarian workmates in our prayer diaries. There may be times when it is not easy for us to talk to them about Jesus, but we can always talk to Jesus about them. When we do so, he may well create opportunities for us to help them in one way or another, and at the right time, speak to them about the one who matters most in our lives.

Finally, we must *love* these non-Christian people we know and meet every day, whether they belong to another religion or not. Jesus loved people however they responded to his message. He looked with infinite compassion on the rich young ruler (Mark 10:21) even though he knew the morally upright, materially prosperous man was going to turn away from Jesus, clutching his god, the money in his swollen purse. But Jesus did not stop loving him because he was not likely to become a convert. We must love as Jesus loved, for love's sake, not just to obtain quick visible results.

Confession of Jesus as uniquely the Son of God is not simply a verbal exercise, said in a sentence, as Nathanael did so movingly when he first met with Christ. It demands our adoration as well as our belief, our worship as well as our witness.

Israel's king

Nathanael made one further affirmation on the day when he openly confessed his personal faith in Christ as his Teacher and God's Son. "You are the King of Israel", he said (1:49). That majestic theme of Christ's kingly rule is declared here but not greatly developed in this gospel until its closing chapters. The title makes a brief but significant appearance in John's Palm Sunday narrative when the same confession as that made personally by Nathanael is made publicly by the crowds thronging the streets of Jerusalem: "Blessed is the king of Israel" (12:13, 15). He was the predicted king of Old Testament prophecy, the promised ruler of Zechariah's message way back in the times when, newly returned from exile, the Israelite people eagerly looked for security and stability (Zechariah 9:9–10). In the terms of that prophecy, he was to be a gentle personality ("riding on a colt, the foal of a donkey"), a morally impeccable ("righteous"), peace-loving Victor who would "take away the chariots from Ephraim and the war horses from Jerusalem". He was to come as the universal Saviour whose "rule will extend from sea to sea".

It is, however, in John's story of the Cross that the kingship theme returns with such persuasive eloquence. This is the gospel where even Pilate, the weak, hesitant, finally compromising unbeliever, refuses to modify the words of that intentionally jocular title which was nailed above Jesus as he died on the Cross: "Jesus of Nazareth, the King of the Jews" (19:19). Yes, Nazareth again, the name which caused Nathanael to make his initially cynical response. Now there were other scoffers, with louder voices and more painful derision than anything of which Nathanael was capable. It is the same dismissive mockery though, but now on the lips of those who respond differently from Nathanael. These people have seen the "greater things" Nathanael was promised (1:50) but they still do not believe. They taunted, even hated, the king. That kingship theme at the close of the gospel is important for us as we think about Nathanael's confession. John alone introduces us to the king's searching question, unique mandate, and eternal destiny.

In this gospel we read first about the king's searching question. Here Pilate interrogates Jesus, "Are you the King of the Jews?" (18:33), but in reply Jesus dares to ask his judge one of life's most penetrating questions, and one which has lost nothing of its challenge with the passing of the years: "Is that your own idea" Jesus asked Pilate, "or did others talk to you about me?" (18:34). That word of the king comes freshly to us, and every disciple. "Is that your own idea" or do you have a second-hand faith, a borrowed faith, an impersonal faith, which has been handed on to you by your parents, or your fellow church attenders? Or is it a vibrant faith which, by personal response to the Gospel, you have made essentially your own? That question is still on the lips of Jesus, and every would-be disciple must have a personal faith as opposed to an inherited one. Jesus rules the kingdom of faith.

Moreover, it is in this gospel that we hear about the king's unique mandate: "My kingdom is not of this world . . . my kingdom is from another place" (18:36–37). Jesus lets Pilate know that he has not been travelling around the country trying to unsettle the Romans. Judea's governor has nothing to fear from Christ. He is not a revolutionary zealot, but a spiritual pioneer. He is about to do something which no human ruler could possibly do. As God's only Son he is going to bear in his sinless and spotless body the sins of the whole world (1:29). Christ's kingdom is not like earthly kingdoms, dependent on political structures, economic stability, military protection. Jesus rules the kingdom of heaven; it consists of heavenly members, whose names are "enrolled" there (Hebrews 12:23), people with heavenly values and heavenly ambitions.

But, although it is "not of this world" that does not mean for a moment that it will not influence this world. It most certainly will. Its message will transform lives, determine values, raise standards, and condemn wrongs. During the dark days of Nonconformist persecution in the late seventeenth-century, many were imprisoned for their faith. In their bewildering adversity heaven became more of an immediate experience than a distant prospect. The presence of Christ their king was so real to these prisoners that they made a serene heaven in an earthly hell. Even in the loneliness of St Nicholas island, off Plymouth, George Hughes can write to his son, incarcerated elsewhere in the same prison: "I am well, and best of all in heaven; and satisfied with the will of God, which will bring us to glory.' One of their leaders, John Howe, said, "It will never be well till our own souls be a heaven to us . . . Bear yourself as an inhabitant of a better country", and Matthew Henry delighted in quoting his father Philip's saying that "All who would go to heaven when they die must begin their heaven while they live". That is exactly the kind of thing that Jesus was saying when he told Pilate that his kingdom was "not of this world". It was not escapism; it was spiritual realism and eternal optimism combined.

This gospel's Passion narrative also reminds us of the king's eternal destiny. Jesus said to Pilate, "You are right in saying I am a king. In fact, for this reason I was born, and for this I came into the world, to testify to the truth" (18:37). The king has defined his kingdom negatively ("not of this world"); now he expounds it positively. It is the kingdom of truth. "Everyone on the side of truth listens to me", says Jesus to his human judge. In that moment, Pilate is confronted with decision, is he for Jesus or against him? He evades the moment of commitment by a cynical aside, "What is truth?" His opportunity had gone, and it was scarcely likely to return.

Nathanael's Teacher desired his obedience. God's Son demanded his worship. Israel's king deserved his service. When Nathanael made that confession on his first encounter with Jesus he was saying that Christ could have the whole of his life and use it in whatever way he felt right. It was a confession which involved him in total surrender. He was openly acknowledging the Crown Rights of his Redeemer. He was responding to Christ's invitation with an eager "I will".

In the late nineteenth century, when the American evangelist D. L. Moody conducted his last mission in London, one of the young stewards in the Metropolitan Tabernacle was a young Pastor's College student, F. W. Boreham. In later life, Boreham described those meetings, and particularly the way in which Moody invited people publicly and verbally to declare their allegiance to Christ:

"Now, who will trust the Saviour here and now? If you will, stand up and say so! Spring to your feet and call out, 'I will!' "

It was a bold thing to ask and it required courage to do it. But people did so, night after night. "The response was sometimes like a clap of thunder", Boreham said. "The effect was electrifying. It was this habit of Mr Moody's that inspired the hymn that was so often sung at the meetings:

> And now, O Lord, give all with us today,
>   The grace to join our song
> And from the heart to gladly with us say:
>   I WILL to Christ belong.
> I will! I will! I will! I will!
>   I will, God helping me, I will, O Lord, be thine,
> Thy precious blood was shed to purchase me –
>   I will be wholly Thine!

The day when Nathanael made his public response to Jesus was the occasion when he said his own "I will". He acknowledged his willingness to learn, his eagerness to worship and his readiness to serve. Christ, his Teacher, God and King, had won this disciple's total allegiance. But the Lord did something more than inspire Nathanael's confession; he widened his horizons. "You shall see greater things", said Jesus. In writing this gospel, John says, "He then *added*, 'I tell you the truth, you shall see heaven open and the angels of God ascending and descending on the Son of Man' ". What Jesus "added" was of the greatest importance, and we must look at his words more closely in our next chapter.

---

1 *Scientology: What is it?* The Church of Scientology International, Los Angeles 1985
2 *ECKENKAR A Way of Life: Book Catalog*, Menlo Park, CA, USA 1982

3 Eileen Barker, *New Religious Movements, A Practical Introduction*, London, Her Majesty's Stationery Office 1989

8

HEAVEN OPEN

JESUS RECOGNIZED that Nathanael's confession was utterly genuine but inadequately based. Looking at him, the Lord said, "You believe because I told you I saw you under the fig tree. You shall see greater things than that." Nathanael had publicly acknowledged the uniqueness of Christ because of something Jesus had revealed to him about himself. Now the Lord tells his newly-enlisted disciple of something "greater" than that – not simply what Jesus knew about Nathanael but what Nathanael could know about Christ.

Jesus then looked to the other people who were standing alongside and, addressing them *all*, said: "I tell you the truth, you shall (all) see heaven open, and the angels of God ascending and descending on the Son of Man."

With this arresting word-picture of an open heaven, Jesus was declaring four things of importance not only for Nathanael but for every Christian disciple. He was saying that "God has given" (that, you will remember, is the meaning of the name "Nathanael") every man and woman four of life's "greater things" in the message of the open heaven: heaven is secure, truth is revealed, sinners are welcomed, and Jesus is glorified.

Heaven is secure

"You shall see heaven open. . . ." In this moment Jesus points away from this world to the next, from the present life to the one that is to come. It is a deliberate declaration at the beginning of this gospel of a truth which frequently recurs in the teaching of the Lord Jesus, that the Gospel is not just about our immediate, present existence but about the future God has prepared for us. Two aspects of that truth are given special prominence in "John": Heaven can begin "now", and heaven is better "then". In this Gospel heaven is both a present possession and an assured future; it can begin *now*, and it will be better *then*.

First, heaven can begin *now*. The Gospel is God's offer in Christ of "eternal life", and this gospel emphatically asserts that "eternal life" is not simply "life after death" but is a quality of life which begins here and now in this life. Let us see how Jesus expounded this message of "eternal life" as a present possession.

He says it is a *transformed* life. It is not a heavenly life which commences when we die; it begins at the moment we put our trust in the Christ who died for us. Jesus made that very plain: "I tell you the truth, whoever hears my word and believes on him who sent me has eternal life and will not be condemned; he has crossed over from death to life" (5:24). That is, for the Christian believer, the moment of radical transition is not the time of dying but the moment of believing.

It is therefore an *imperishable* life. It will last for ever.

This, surely, is one of the "heavenly things" which Jesus longs to share with Nicodemus (3:12) – the assurance that those who believe in Jesus will never perish but have eternal life (3:16). Jesus said that the Israelite pilgrims who ate the miraculous manna every day of their journey, still died in the wilderness, but those who receive Christ, "the bread of life" will never die eternally. They may pass through the experience of physical death (unless Christ comes again in their lifetime) but they will never know what it is to experience eternal death, or separation from God (6:48–51).

It is a *forgiven* life; even though they have transgressed, those who trust Christ as their Saviour from sin are found guilty and mercifully acquitted (3:17). In contrast, those who refuse to accept Christ's offer of eternal life will certainly be condemned at the bar of God's judgment because they have thereby committed the most serious of all sins. Their offence is far more serious than that of theft, murder, adultery, and so on – it is the alarming sin of deliberate and persistent Christ-rejection: "Whoever rejects the Son will not see life, for God's wrath remains on him" (3:36).

It is an *assured* life. Nobody need be in the slightest doubt about its possession. Jesus clearly said, "Whoever believes in the Son *has* eternal life" (3:36). That certainly is conveyed through Christ's teaching in this gospel with persuasive clarity.

It is a *satisfying* life. On one occasion the people who were listening to Jesus asked him to give them another miraculous sign so that they might be fully persuaded that he was the promised Messiah. He had only just fed a huge crowd of people from the one slender lunch of a young lad, but the people wanted further evidence of his uniqueness. Jesus knew that people would not be persuaded about his deity no matter how many miracles he performed. The crowds knew that there were stories going about that when the Messiah came he would produce bread from heaven as Moses had in the desert. Jesus said that the manna in the wilderness was only a foreshadowing of the eternal food they would receive in him. "I am the bread of life. He who comes to me will never go hungry, and he who believes in me will never be thirsty" (6:35).

It is a *secure* life. Jesus said that those who possess God's gift of eternal life are eternally safe and secure. It is impossible for them to be lost. "And this is the will of him who sent me, that I shall lose none of all that he has given me, but raise them up at the last day" (6:39, 44).

All this is arrestingly conveyed by Jesus as truth which the believer possesses here and now in this present life. To have "eternal life" is to enter into the enjoyment and security of these realities in this present world.

Secondly, heaven will be better *then*. At a time when Jesus was speaking to his disciples about his own impending death and their consequent danger, he went on to tell them about the place he was going to prepare for us in heaven (14:1-2). Jesus is telling his followers that when the moment comes for his arrest and crucifixion, when all seems most dark and when they may be tempted to utter despair, "*keep on believing* in God", (that is the force of the verb here), keep on believing that he is sovereign and working out his all-wise plan of salvation, even through these awful circumstances of Good Friday. Moreover, Jesus says, "*keep on believing* in me", even though everything you see and hear appears to contradict this great truth of my deity and saving work. "Keep on believing that, even in such a physically devastating and spiritually

bewildering context, I am fulfilling God's redemptive purposes and will be going ahead of you into that safe eternity
which I will be preparing for you and for all who trust
me as Saviour and Lord."

Across the centuries, Christian believers have rejoiced
in this great truth. Heaven is open for them because of
what Jesus has done for them on the Cross. Easter Day
and Ascension Day mean that he has opened for us our
eternal heaven. We know that when we die physically, we
will go to be with our Lord for ever. There may well be
moments in the life of any Christian when he or she begins
to waver on the reality of heaven. It is therefore of the
greatest importance that we remember the context in
which Jesus spelt out the certainty of heaven — not in the
bright sunshine of successful days of public ministry, but
when the dark clouds were gathering. He shared this confidence and urged us to *keep on believing* in him when he
was facing his own death.

The chapter divisions in the Bible sometimes rob a
saying of its context in the ministry of Jesus. For that
reason, the familiar and reassuring opening verses of John
14 need to be seen in their original setting. When he talked
about our heavenly home it was in the context of his own
impending execution. He could look beyond the experience of dying to the moment when he would be raised
from the dead, and enter heaven for us. His own death
was surrounded by desperate sadness. Jesus had just been
predicting the tragic circumstances of his betrayal by one
of his own followers. Whilst he was speaking about such
an awful thing, he was, understandably, *"troubled* in
spirit"* (13:21). He used the same word earlier when he
was anticipating his own sacrificial death, "Now my heart
is *troubled"* (12:27), and John uses it in this gospel to

describe the emotional reaction of Jesus when he was in the presence of two bereaved people: "he was deeply moved in spirit and *troubled*" (11:33). Then, that same word "troubled" is, once again, on the lips of Jesus as he talks to his disciples about their death as well as his own: "Let not your hearts be *troubled* . . . keep on believing in me".

When this gospel of John first began to circulate among the churches of the first-century world, a number of its readers knew that they might also face death in humanly agonizing circumstances. Jesus warned his followers that if he had been persecuted, they must not imagine that they would escape it (15:18–20; 16:2–4, 33). The Epilogue to this gospel preserves the prediction of Jesus that Peter would suffer martyrdom and, as an older man, would be carried where, humanly speaking, he did not wish to go — to the place of execution (21:18–19). But, like every other disciple, Peter could be assured of a secure place in heaven, and die in the certainty that the Lord of Life was waiting there to welcome him home.

In our late-twentieth-century world, death is an unmentionable topic. If it happens to emerge in conversation, it is quickly dismissed as a morbid, unwelcome theme. But Christians who take the message of Jesus seriously are not afraid of death. They recall that he talked about it not as a terminus but as a transition, not as a dreaded end but as a gloriously new beginning. The well-known evangelist Lindsay Glegg used to treasure a postcard which had been sent to him by the famous Baptist preacher, F. B. Meyer, only a few days before his death. In a shaky hand, Meyer wrote these words: "I have raced you to heaven. I am just off; see you there, Love, F. B. Meyer."[1]

That is the confidence which is given to those who "keep on believing" in what Jesus promised about the life to come. The one who said, "I am ... the truth" would hardly have told Nathanael that he would see heaven open if such a place did not exist. He was describing something more than the clouds; he was telling his new disciple about a life beyond this one, and a better one too. But the message of an "open heaven" is saying something else as well.

Truth is revealed

When the Jewish rabbis spoke about heaven being "open", they sometimes used the expression metaphorically to express the idea that God had parted the heavens to share truth with them. They worshipped a "God in heaven who reveals mysteries" (Daniel 2:28) and believed that God was pleased to unfold his message to those who had eyes to see and ears to hear it. Jesus may also have been telling Nathanael that he would gradually see for himself something greater than what he had just discerned, that Jesus knew all about him. Along with his fellow-disciples in every century, he would come to grasp great biblical truths for himself and have the grace to apply them to his life. The truth of God would leap from the pages of Scripture for him, just as they had spoken so forcefully, through Moses and the prophets, to his friend Philip.

That has certainly happened to Christ's disciples in every century. As they have read the Scriptures, heaven has been opened for them. Sometimes in the moment of extreme despair, when everything seemed too much for them, God has, as it were, parted the heavens, to give them a clear view of some great truth which has changed their lives completely. It was like that for Luther in the sixteenth century. This is how he describes the "open heaven" for him, his experience of God's revelation of truth as, in great despair, he read from Paul's letter to the Romans. Initially, what he saw, the truth about himself, grieved him, but then he came to see the truth about God's gift of righteousness, and that healed him. He felt as though he had entered "paradise itself". Heaven was open.

> Though I lived as a monk without reproach, I felt that I was a sinner before God with an extremely disturbed conscience. I could not believe that he was placated by my satisfaction. I did not love, yes I hated the righteous God who punished sinners, and secretly, if not blasphemously, certainly murmuring greatly. I was angry with God . . .
>
> At last, by the mercy of God, meditating day and night, I gave heed to the context of the words, namely, "In it the righteousness of God is revealed, as it is written, 'He who through faith is righteous shall live'". There I began to understand that . . . the righteousness of God is revealed by the gospel, namely, the passive righteousness with which a merciful God justifies us by faith, as it is written, "He who through faith is righteous shall live".
>
> Here I felt that I was altogether born again and had entered paradise itself through open gates.

Luther came to see that other passages of Scripture did not simply describe God's nature and attributes but also spoke convincingly in the same places of God's work in us as, for example, "the power of God, with which he makes us strong, the wisdom of God, with which he makes us wise".[2]

This gospel of John emphasizes the importance of truth.

Christ is the truth for the world (1:14; 14:6). He brought
the truth to the world (1:17; 18:37) and speaks the truth
in the world (1:51; 3:3; 5:19). He describes the Spirit of
truth (14:17; 16:13) and sends the Spirit of truth (15:26).
By this truth believers are liberated (8:32) and sanctified
(17:17). Heaven is open not only for Luther but for everyone who listens to Jesus as the Holy Spirit seeks to make
him known (15:26).

This is a necessary word for times like our own when
authority is challenged, faith ridiculed, standards lowered,
values ignored, and convictions despised. Christian truth
is hastily dismissed as an irrelevant aspect of distant
antiquity. The scepticism is not peculiar to the Christian
tradition nor to the United Kingdom. The Chief Rabbi
tells us that in a recent survey among American Jews, two-
thirds *disagreed* with the statement that "To be a good
Jew one must believe in God".[3] For such people, "Jewish-
ness" has lost all meaningful contact with its biblical roots.
The Old Testament is as irrelevant to them as is the New
for many nominal "Christians". The tag is used simply to
distinguish them from "pagans" but it bears no resem-
blance whatever to its original usage.

So, in the contemporary scene, it is all the more important that Christian truth be loyally and lovingly shared.
Our neigbours have little notion as to what Christians
really believe, and the television debate or newspaper
report may suggest that they no longer believe in anything
very much. These are times of widespread spiritual ignorance and, if heaven is to be "opened" for some of the
people we meet every day, then Christian hearts must
be compassionately opened as we believers realize that
our unconverted friends are destined for a Christless
eternity. And lips must be fearlessly opened so that those

unbelievers we meet will at least know what God thinks about human indifference, about what it means to be a Christian and why Christ died to make that miracle possible.

Sinners are welcomed

There was, therefore, another aspect of vital truth about "greater things" that Jesus shared that day with Nathanael. It was this distinctive message which all disciples must personally appropriate and eagerly share: sinful men and women can be eternally forgiven. The vision at Bethel centuries before (Genesis 28:10–17) was surely intended to assure Jacob that, however serious and sickening his transgression, it had not cut him off from a compassionate God. Here was a stairway to God; the way was open into his merciful presence. Why did the angels figure so prominently in Jacob's dream? Remember that the word "angel" simply means "messenger". God was sending to Jacob this message of generous forgiveness by a descending angel, in the hope that an ascending angel would one day convey the prayer of a penitent Jacob. Though by his sin Jacob had offended God, grieved his father and alienated his brother, the way was still open into the presence of a loving God.

Jesus was telling Nathanael that he would witness something far greater that Jacob's vision – not simply a visual portrait of a stairway with angelic traffic touching the life of one solitary patriarch, but a means of access to God through Christ for everyone throughout the world who genuinely believes. This is a far "greater thing": there is an open way of communication between heaven and earth.

Through Jesus God was conveying to sinful mankind his most persuasive message. It was not only Jacob the cunning sinner who was to see "the stairway resting on the earth with its top reaching to heaven". Throughout the centuries, millions of others would come to realize that:

> There is a way for man to rise
> To that sublime abode;
> An offering and a sacrifice,
> A Holy Spirit's energies,
> An Advocate with God.

Others, like Nathanael and Luther and millions more, would also be welcomed as forgiven sinners. The "stairway" of Jacob's dream is transformed into a reality greater by far, from something to Someone – the Saviour himself. The angels of God are "ascending and descending on the Son of Man". It was the Lord Jesus who would make possible this essential traffic from earth to heaven. By him alone, men and women would be reconciled to God. If Jacob, the deceitful schemer, the cruel thief, the runaway rogue, could be forgiven, then so could anyone. Elizabeth Clephane captured the theme beautifully in her magnificent hymn, "Beneath the Cross of Jesus":

> As to the holy patriarch
> That wondrous dream was given
> So seems my Saviour's cross to me
> A ladder up to heaven.

We recall that in this gospel of John, Christ is portrayed as the Lamb of God who takes away the sin of the world (1:29). If it is for "the world", nobody need feel too bad for this forgiveness, and nobody dare feel too good for it either. The death of Christ was not a sacrifice necessary only for blatant and notorious sinners. When he was "lifted up from the earth", he said it was so that he could "draw all men to myself" (12:32). It encompasses all.

Nobody is beyond the reach of that saving Cross. In this gospel the immoral Samaritan is forgiven (4:16–17, 29); the new well of life-giving water springs up within her, washing away her evident, public sin. But it is not simply for Samaritan outcasts. Later in the gospel, a Jewish offender is also forgiven. She has broken the Law of Moses. That Law says she should die, but grace says that she may live. Those around her were fierce in their condemnation, ready to kill her for the offence of adultery. But Jesus forgives her and tells her to leave her "life of sin" once and for all (8:11). The Light of the World had shone into the dark recesses of her unclean lifestyle, and she is determined never again to "walk in darkness" but have "the light of life" (8:12).

Moreover, it is not only blatantly immoral offenders who need the forgiveness of Christ. So do his best disciples. They need to be cleansed and forgiven for their arrogant pride (13:8), empty words (13:37), hasty temper (18:10), appalling cowardice (18:15–18, 25–27), and aloof unbelief (20:24–27). And pardoned they were. They too knew the experience of an open heaven and, once made clean, were sent out with the message that others could also be forgiven, on the authority of the Risen Christ's unchanging promise (20:23).

In every century men and women have blessed God for that open heaven. Burdened about his sin, the young George Fox went to one minister after another but "saw they were all miserable comforters". But a day came when he too had a vision of an open heaven:

> At another time I saw the great love of God, and I
> was filled with admiration at the infiniteness of it;
> and then I saw . . . what entered into God's kingdom,
> and how by Jesus the opener of the door by his
> heavenly key, the entrance was given . . . My living
> faith was raised that I saw all was done by Christ,
> the life, and my belief was in him.[4]

Fox realized that "seeing" Jesus in heaven as "the opener
of the door" causes us to look away from anything on
earth as the means of our salvation. The "greater things"
include the open heaven of our salvation. To look up to
that heaven is to look away from ourselves. It is to realize
that salvation is not to be achieved by our own efforts in
this world, our moral striving, or our religious attain-
ments. If we are to be changed by Jesus we must recognize
that these things cannot change dishonest cheats like Jacob
and proud cynics like Nathanael. If heaven is to be opened
for us eternally then we must look up now, and place our
hope in Christ alone.

But our great mistake in the late-twentieth-century
world is to look elsewhere for our salvation. Help from
outside is the last thing we need. Surely all the resources
for self-improvement are at our disposal? Yet how can we
continue to believe such an insubstantial myth in a world
which, they tell us, has only had one peaceful day since
the end of the Second World War? That is, throughout
these decades, violence and aggression on a large scale
have shattered the peace in some part or other of the world
on every single day but one. In his 1990 Reith Lectures,
Jonathan Sacks made the point that "the self-perfectibility
of man" is "the greatest illusion of modern times". Yet,
how arrogant were our dreams. Things were bound to get

better, and who needs God when people can manage so extremely well on their own?

Sacks observes that in the immediate post-war era, people genuinely believed that "science would fathom the mysteries of nature, and technology would harvest its treasures. Reason would give place to superstition, and tolerance would triumph over prejudice. The modern state would bring participation and equality. The individual would have freedom of choice, freed from paternalist authority".

But, says Jonathan Sacks, "at some stage in the 1960s, profound doubts began to be expressed. Technology had given us the power to destroy life on earth. Economic growth was consuming the environment. The modern state had the power to organize tyranny and violence on a scale hitherto unknown. Racial animosities had not disappeared: they had fired the ovens of Auschwitz. No Utopia had yet been brought by revolution, and the free market was increasing the inequalities between rich and poor. In the secular city there was homelessness and violence, and individualism had made the most basic relationships vulnerable."

Robert Bellah expressed the disillusionment perfectly when he said: "Progress, modernity's master idea, seems less compelling when it appears that it may be progress into the abyss."[5]

Jesus points away from the "abyss" to the "above". Philip discovers truth from above (1:45). Nathanael finds grace from above. Nicodemus hears of life from above (3:3). The crowds are told of food from above (6:32–35), light from above (8:12), hope from above (11:25–26). Peter needs cleansing from above (13:6–10), Thomas faith from above (20:26–28). This gospel is constantly reminding its readers that those who genuinely long to be different must begin by looking away from themselves. An open heaven is the only hope for a disillusioned world. It was Francis Thompson who reminded us that Christ is near if only we will look, but all too often our "estranged faces . . . miss the many-splendoured thing":

> O world invisible, we view thee,
> O world intangible, we touch thee,
> O world unknowable, we know thee,
> Inapprehensible, we clutch thee!

Humanly speaking, Thompson's life was a failure. Destined for the priesthood, he was judged to be without a true vocation. Turning from theological studies, he began to read medicine but failed to qualify as a doctor. In 1885 he left home, and spent three homeless years in London, dependent on opium, and destitute. A drug addict longing to be different, Thompson comes to portray the immediacy of this open heaven:

> But (when so sad thou canst not sadder)
> Cry, – and upon thy so sore loss
> Shall shine the traffic of Jacob's ladder
> Pitched between Heaven and Charing Cross.
>
> Yea, in the night, my Soul, my daughter,
> Cry – clinging Heaven by the hems;
> And lo, Christ walking on the water
> Not of Gennesareth, but Thames![6]

Jesus is glorified

A further truth remains. The open heaven reveals the unique Son of Man, ascended and exalted. It is a portrait of triumphant victory. In this saying about "greater things" we are told, right at the beginning of this gospel, that Jesus will complete his work on earth, his saving sacrifice, be raised from the dead and enter his glory: "You shall see heaven open . . . and . . . the Son of Man". This saving truth belongs, most of all, to the "greater things" Nathanael will live to see fulfilled in Jesus. Nathanael has confessed the deity of Christ. To perceive that truth is surely a "gift of God". Here Jesus tells his disciple that in addition to being the conquering "Son of God" arrestingly described in some of the great Psalms (2:7–9), he is also the compassionate "Son of Man" from Daniel's prophecy. Daniel's portrait from the dark days of exile certainly depicts a mighty Victor who rules over an everlasting dominion (Daniel 7:13–14) but it also reminds us that there is a Man in heaven, one "able to sympathize with our weaknesses" (Hebrew 4:15).

During his earthly ministry Jesus would be criticized, slandered, pursued, misunderstood, ridiculed, dismissed, and forsaken, but right at the beginning he told Nathanael and the others standing by that they would all see the day when he would become the exalted Lord of glory. Heaven would be open and, looking up, men and women throughout the world would acknowledge his deity, receive his truth, and appropriate his power.

As if to demonstrate the proximity of these "greater things" to Nathanael especially, the scene moves directly from this saying of Jesus (1:51) to Nathanael's home town, Cana of Galilee (2:1). This gospel makes a special point of telling us where Nathanael came from (21:2), and also that Cana was the place where Christ's first two "signs" take place. One was the miracle of the transformed water and the other the miracle of the restored youth. Those are the key themes here – transformation and restoration. That is how Christ "revealed his glory" and inspired confidence in those who had begun to follow him (2:11). Cana was a small community. These people were Nathanael's neighbours. They knew that he had confessed the Sonship and Kingship of Christ. It was as if, in the homes of Cana, Jesus wanted not only to unveil his own glory but encourage this new disciple's faith. Heaven was opening already. Needs were met and lives were changed.

The first sign (2:1–11), the changing of the water into wine, met a perceived material need. There was no wine. All the resources had been totally exhausted. In desperation, Mary comes to Jesus to make the need known. Even as he responds in love, he tells her that, whatever he may do, a "greater thing" is on the horizon: "My time has not yet come." But she urges the servants to "do whatever he tells you". The miracle will be effected by a word: "Fill the jars with water . . . Now draw some out and take it to the master of the banquet." That uniquely powerful Word, which had effected miracles at the Creation (1:3) was at work again on earth. It was saying in unmistakable terms that life's most drab, difficult, unexpected, embarrassing, frustrating circumstances can be totally changed by the power of the glorified Christ.

The second sign (4:46–54) also began within the community at Cana. In compiling this gospel, John wants us to see both miracles alongside each other, and it looks as if even their geographical location is of some importance: "Once more he visited Cana in Galilee, where he had turned the water into wine." A nobleman from Capernaum had hurried specially to the town to see Jesus. There was little hope for his dying son. Once again, human resources are totally exhausted. Yet, the nobleman argued, a man who can change water into wine is surely capable of turning sickness into health. But, he pondered, Jesus worked the miracle at Cana's wedding reception because he was actually there among the guests that day. But Jesus is not in Capernaum; he is 20 miles away at Cana: "Come down before my child dies." Christ was eager to respond to deep human need and to this man's expressed faith. He wanted to demonstrate beyond all doubt that his physical presence was not a condition of his miraculous power. "The man took Jesus at his word . . . Then the father realized that this was the exact time at which Jesus had said to him, 'Your son will live.'" It was the word that did the work.

Both miracles created faith. After what happened at the wedding, "the first of his miraculous signs" caused his disciples to "put their faith in him". When the nobleman got back to Capernaum and found his son released from the fever from the very moment Jesus had spoken the liberating word, "he and all his household believed" (4:53). This "second miraculous sign that Jesus performed" had also brought needy people to the place of grateful confession. Like Nathanael they had met the Son of Man. The contexts were different – the happy, carefree guests at Cana's marriage feast, and the distressed family at Capernaum, anxiously caring for a dying boy. But, in Christ, God had stepped into both homes. Both families had seen heaven open, and life for them would never be the same again. More important by far – Jesus had been glorified.

1 John Fear, ed., *The Best in Life: Selections from the ministry of A. Lindsay Glegg*, Word Books 1972, 123
2 Luther, Preface to Latin Writings, 1545, in John Dillenberger ed., *Martin Luther: Selections from his writings*, Anchor Books, New York 1961, 11
3 Jonathan Sacks, *The Persistence of Faith: Religion, Morality and Society in a Secular Age*, The Reith Lectures 1990, Weidenfeld and Nicolson 1991, 7
4 John L. Nickalls, ed., *The Journal of George Fox*, 1975, 13–14
5 Jonathan Sacks, *The Persistence of Faith*, 76–77
6 Francis Thompson, "The Kingdom of God: In no strange land"

9

BREAD ENOUGH AND TO SPARE

WE HAVE SEEN THAT, following Nathanael's confession, Jesus performed two signs in his home town of Cana in Galilee. It was as if, from the start, Jesus wanted to encourage Nathanael's faith on his own home ground, so that his friends and neighbours would see that the heaven had truly opened for this devout follower of Jesus. John tells us that Andrew and Philip both belonged to Bethsaida (1:44) and when, in his travels, Jesus reached their home territory he did much the same for them.

John records the story of this sign, the feeding of the multitude (6:1–15), and tells us that this miraculous event took place on "the far shore of the Sea of Galilee". Luke (9:10–17) identifies the name of the place where it all happened, Bethsaida, the native town of the two disciples. John alone records that on this memorable occasion both disciples had something to say to Jesus and the occurrence of their names together invites us to turn again to this familiar narrative. We do so with one purpose in mind — to look at six vivid portraits of Jesus which emerge in its story.

Nobody can hope to be an effective disciple without a

renewed awareness of the greatness of Christ. At the end of that day when the thousands were fed, Andrew and Philip both emerged from the scene with an enlarged vision of Jesus. They saw him that day as they had never seen him before, and the impression was unforgettable. We too need big portraits of Christ if we are to live and work effectively for Christ in a godless society. If our vision of Christ is not constantly enlarged and our understanding of him perpetually enriched, we shall end up with a decrepit faith and a diminished witness.

Andrew and Peter had been called to discipleship by Jesus. Both had followed him but, the day the thousands were fed at Bethsaida, both disciples discovered new things about the compassionate, sovereign, dependent, sufficient, sympathetic and surrendered Christ.

The compassionate Christ

He anticipates needs. When Jesus looked up he was conscious of the people's physical, material, intellectual and spiritual needs.

First of all, the Lord was sensitive to the people's physical needs. John tells us that the great crowds which pressed towards Bethsaida that day were following Jesus because "they saw the miraculous signs he had performed on the sick". They were aware of his immense compassion for men and women who were unwell, and in that crowd there must have been large numbers of people who were struggling physically to make the journey – disabled people who were only in the crowd because their friends were willing to carry them on a stretcher. In such a huge crowd there must have been deaf men and women who could not hear the excited conversation of their fellow-travellers, eagerly sharing news of Christ's latest miraculous healing. Dumb people were there with no ability to ask how far they might have to go before they could come face to face with the healing Christ. Blind people were groping their way along the dusty roads, thronged with determined travellers. Lepers may even have lingered behind at a safe distance. John would hardly have said that the crowds followed because of the healing miracles of Jesus if the sick had not been present. People were there who were not simply present out of curiosity about what he had done for others, but because of what he might do for them. The long, tiring day in the sweltering heat was abundantly worthwhile if at the end of that journey Christ could meet their deep, personal physical needs. Matthew tells us that Jesus used this very occasion to minister to people who were unwell. Before he fed the hungry "he had compassion on them and healed their sick" (Matthew 14:14).

Jesus knows all about our material needs as well. He was concerned about the increasing hunger of such a vast crowd and for that reason addressed his searching question to Philip: "Where shall we buy bread for these people to eat?" Even the healthy were hungry, and it was humanly impossible to meet the material needs of several thousand people. Only the compassionate Christ could do that. In today's global village, no Christian can be complacent in the light of the immense problem of world hunger. With such a huge capacity for practical compassion, Jesus would have been deeply moved by the sight of what we see from time to time, as close as our television screens. No believer can possibly maintain his love for Christ and at the same time be indifferent to those hungry millions who are loved by him in the deprived areas of the Third World. It must surely drive us to some kind of action. We can give, and need to do so regularly, possibly by donating the money we would have spent on at least one main meal a week. We must be informed so that we know specific areas of world need and can press for appropriate action by governments. We should pray, for the Lord longs that we share our burden for them with him, and we can encourage others to have a similar concern. Perhaps we ought to volunteer to do something practical by way of helping others to see these needs, or by volunteering some part-time help with one of the main Christian relief organizations.

Tear Fund, for example, offers excellent opportunities for people who can give some time as short-term workers. There's a wide variety of different opportunities in various parts of the world. Some people may be able to give a few weeks in the summer, others may be in a position to offer a whole year. There are summer projects in Africa, Asia, Central or South America, with jobs like building a hospital ward, painting a school, or capping a well. Those who are able to give a longer period, like a year, will naturally be people with practical training in health-care, agriculture, forestry, engineering, administration, and various trades. Is the Lord asking you to share his concern for the needy people of his world?

Jesus was aware of their intellectual needs. The story says that Jesus "went up on a mountainside and sat down with his disciples". The Jewish rabbi always "sat down" in order to teach his eager disciples; it was the recognized posture of the authentic teacher, and here Jesus was about to give instruction to his chosen team of learners. Mark's account of the story actually says that, prior to the miraculous meal, Jesus "began teaching them many things"

(6:34). Jesus knows that we need something more than physical health and material food. Our minds need to be fed. We need the truth of God which alone will meet the deepest of life's needs.

This story shows that Jesus knows our spiritual needs also. He did not only address the huge crowds (Mark 6:34), or the more restricted group of disciples (John 6:3). He also spoke personally to one disciple, eager to use the occasion to assess Philip's spiritual development and at least increase one disciple's maturity. Jesus did that because he loved Philip and wanted his disciple to be at his best spiritually. He believed in the importance of one-to-one teaching, personal involvement with specific human needs, and sensitive pastoral care. He wanted to know how Philip as an individual was getting on spiritually, and so he put the question to him about buying the bread for the people to eat. But, John tells us, Jesus only made the enquiry "to test him". He wanted to know how Philip thought the needs might be met. Philip made a rough calculation as to the number of people who were there, and then hazarded a guess as to how much it would cost just to provide an inadequate snack. It would use up eight months' wages, and who had that kind of money handy anyway?

Andrew at least drew attention to the little meal they did have rather than the necessary money they didn't have. But he too succumbed to despair: "how far will they go among so many?" But Jesus was using these important preliminary enquiries to enable the disciples to understand their total dependence on him. Like us, they had to be brought to an end of themselves before they could appreci-ate the adequacy of Christ. The seventeenth-century Puri-tan, William Bridge, said, "So long as man can find a fulness in any creature, he comes not to God . . . So long as man has encouragement elsewhere, he does not encourage himself in the Lord his God."[1]

The disciples were made to see the immensity of the problem before they were allowed to witness the magnitude of Christ. If Philip and Andrew had somehow or other gained access to necessary human resources, the miracle would not have happened. It was only when they saw the massive amount that was needed, and the meagre amount that was available, that they realized how hopeless they were to meet the situation without the unique help of Jesus.

But Jesus asked his penetrating question to help Philip reach the heart of the problem, and that demonstrates beyond doubt the intense concern which Christ has in our individual spiritual development. The more we see our need of him, the more we long for him, and the more we reach out to him, the more we grow.

We can see already from the opening sentences of John's dramatic story that, in his immense compassion, Jesus is concerned about us physically, materially, intellectually, and spiritually.

The sovereign Christ

Jesus not only anticipates needs; he controls circumstances. John tells us that when Jesus spoke to Philip about the people's hunger he put the question about the bread "only to test him, for he already had in mind what he was going to do". Christ was perfectly in control of the situation and nothing that happened that day took him by surprise. It was important for the disciples to realize that.

In its presentation of Christ's person, teaching and work, John's gospel perfectly balances the humanity and deity of the Lord Jesus. In this account of his earthly ministry, Jesus is fully human and totally dependent on the Father for everything he says and does, yet at the same time he is equipped with divine qualities and attributes that are characteristic of his unique deity. As the matchless Son of God he is aware of his divinely appointed destiny. He speaks throughout his ministry of that "hour" which awaits him, the time when his life would be offered as a saving sacrifice.

At Cana's wedding, he tells his mother that his hour has not yet come (2:4). Later, he says the same thing to his unbelieving brothers (7:5–6, 8). John tells us that on two occasions when Jesus was in Jerusalem, teaching in the Temple, the authorities would like to have arrested him but did not succeed "because his time had not yet come" (7:30; 8:20). As the time of his appointed destiny drew closer he said, "The hour has come for the Son of Man to be glorified" (12:23, 27). When he met with his disciples at the end he "knew that the time had come for him to leave this world and go to the Father" (13:1). As he drew nearer to the end, he began his prayer of consecration by saying, "Father, the time has come" (17:1).

It is a portrait of a Saviour who is very much in command; nothing is happening to him by chance, and he permits the various events to take place as the hours slip by. Prior to the beginning of the miraculous meal, he knew what he was about to do, and at its close he was similarly in full control. When the enamoured crowd witnessed this astonishing feast, they began to whisper among themselves that surely here was the promised Messiah. Popular legend had it that when the Anointed One came, he would feed the hungry and meet the needs of the destitute. Swayed by the evidence, large numbers of people made their way towards Jesus, determined to recognize him publicly as their appointed leader and liberator. But, says John, long before they took their first steps towards him, Jesus, "knowing that they intended to come and make him king by force, withdrew again to a mountain by himself".

Once again, at the end of the miracle as at its beginning, we see a Lord who is in full control. Philip and his partners came to see that as the weeks and months went by, and later reflected on his unrivalled sovereignty. Throughout the centuries that have followed, believers have rejoiced in the certainty that their lives are in the hands of a Saviour who already has in mind what he is going to do. They have come to see that, under the control of Christ, their lives are not a series of disconnected accidents. Even in moments when we do not discern him to be at work, he most certainly is. In the wide variety of life's circumstances he is there, in one way or another, patiently working out his loving purposes. Sometimes he is testing us, as with Philip, often encouraging us, as with Andrew (1:41–42), frequently correcting us, as with Thomas (20:27), always forgiving us, as with Peter (21:15–19). But, in all these different contexts, he is sovereignly at work, determined to do his utmost for us and bring out the best in us.

In the dark and difficult years of persecution when this gospel was circulated, believers were glad to be assured that even in moments when they were arrested, imprisoned, tortured, even executed, Christ was in control. Across the centuries, many a perplexed and bewildered Christian must have lingered with those words. Rejoicing in the kingly rule of Christ, they have acknowledged with radiant confidence that he already has in mind what he is going to do.

The dependent Christ

Jesus expresses reliance, even in his sovereignty. With matchless artistry, John presents a balanced picture of Christ. Even though he is in full control, he chooses to be fully committed to the Father's will and entirely dependent on the Father's resources for what he says, does, and has. Each is important, for disciples as well as for their Lord.

In this gospel Jesus relies totally on the Father for what he *does*: "The Son can do nothing by himself; he can only do what he sees the Father doing" (5:19–20, 30). Jesus did not want to do anything which was not part of the Father's plan for his life. He insisted on doing only the things which pleased God. That was the refining process through which passed every fresh ambition. Will my Father derive pleasure from what I do in this particular situation? If his pleasure is debatable, the idea is best discarded, and the sooner the better.

Jesus is equally reliant on the Father for what he *says*: "I do nothing on my own but speak just what the Father has taught me" (8:28). Again, "the Father who sent me commanded me what to say, and how to say it" (12:49). That is impressive. Jesus knew that in the art of communication how we say things is as important as what we say. Many a well-meaning person has had the truth of the matter in his mind, but has failed to get it across because it was spoilt by the wrong motivation, or a hostile presentation, or an unloving attitude, or even by careless words.

The ideas were all right but they were clothed in such clumsy language.

Jesus is also dependent on the Father for what he *has*. When this little boy's minute picnic is placed into his sovereign hands, he takes the little loaves and gives thanks. He offers a prayer of profound gratitude to the Father for the limited resources at his disposal, knowing that if it pleased God, they would be abundantly multiplied – and they most certainly were.

Everything possible is done in the narrative to underline the totally inadequate natural provisions, and the Lord's complete reliance on the Father's resources. Look at what is available from a purely human point of view. Here we have a group of despairing disciples, fully agreeing with Andrew and Philip's pessimism: "Eight months' wages would not buy enough . . . how far will they go among so many?" And beside them an insignificant volunteer, a very young boy indeed. The noun used to describe him is a double diminutive. People used the word *pais* to describe a youth, *paidion* for a boy, and *paidarion* for a small boy. And what is in the young boy's hand? A meagre meal indeed, only sufficient for a very young lad. Everything is done to make it clear that we are looking at a tiny offering – here are five *small* loaves and two *small* fish, and the bread is "barley bread", the cheaper food with which the poor were content, whilst people with even modest resources would eat wheat bread. This little boy certainly did not come from an affluent home.

So, there is a deliberate emphasis here on the total inadequacy of human resources, but they are in the hands of a grateful Lord who always looks to his heavenly Father to provide the bread sufficient for each new day. That was how Jesus taught his disciples to pray (Luke 11:3), and that is how he expected them to live – completely reliant on a generous God.

The sufficient Christ

Jesus surpasses expectations. It was not simply that the people had enough to eat. There was more provided than they could possibly eat, and John underlines this in his narrative. They were generously given "as much as they wanted". It was when "they had all had enough to eat" that Jesus talked to them about others.

He always gives more than we need. What he offers is not simply life, but abundant life, life "to the full" (10:10). He promises not peace but "peace which transcends all understanding" (Philippians 4:7). His love defies adequate definition; it "surpasses knowledge" (Ephesians 3:19). His riches are "glorious riches" (Ephesians 3:16). His power is "all-surpassing power" (2 Corinthians 4:7). His grace is totally sufficient (2 Corinthians 12:9).

This is the gospel of lavish abundance. At Cana's wedding feast, the jars were filled to the brim (2:7). The wine is splashing over on to the courtyard floor. If Jesus is to meet human need, he will do it with princely generosity. If hungry people are to be fed in Bethsaida, then there must be plenty for everyone and enough for those who are not present as well as for those who are. Isaac Watts encouraged his contemporaries to sing with joyous thankfulness:

> How vast the treasure we possess!
>   How rich thy bounty, King of grace!
> This world is ours, and worlds to come;
> Earth is our lodge, and heaven our home.

The sympathetic Christ

Jesus considers others. He is pleased when the hungry people enjoy their meal, but his thoughts have already turned towards those who are not sitting on the grassy slope of this hillside. There are hungry people in the surrounding villages and their needs must be met also. "Gather the pieces that are left over. Let nothing be wasted." Twelve tall baskets are borrowed from some nearby homes and in the closing hours of the day, disciples and others are busy, distributing the food to those who had not been able to follow Jesus to Bethsaida. What is this saying to us in our very different world?

It is surely saying that Jesus dislikes waste. Those words, "Let nothing be wasted" ought to be written on a small card and displayed in the kitchen of every Christian in the country. In a world where millions die of starvation every year, it is offensive for some believers to take more than they can possibly eat, or buy that which they have little prospect of using. The world's hungry have to be content with tiny scraps of almost inedible food, whilst the world's rich have problems of obesity, alcoholism, lung cancer and the rest. The Christian's life style needs to be checked constantly against that word of Jesus to his disciples as they collected the abundant leftovers: "Nothing wasted".

It is surely saying that Jesus abhors destitution. The poor people of Galilee were his deep concern that day when they carried the baskets away from the hillside where thousands had eaten their fill. He grieves in today's world when Christians are indifferent to the needs of the poor, the homeless, and the deprived. These are the people who would have been first on his list of compassionate priorities. That is why he sent the broken bread into the

surrounding villages. Yet in our world 250,000 children
will become permanently blinded this year simply for lack
of a vitamin A capsule or a daily handful of green vege-
tables.[2] The sympathetic Christ must be saying something
to his followers in a world where people can become blind
simply because they are poor.

Each year that passes 230,000 children are struck down
by polio because they do not receive the immunization
which has virtually eliminated polio from Western society.
Can the Saviour who loved crippled people be indifferent
to that?

Fourteen million children die every year from common
illnesses and malnutrition. Most could be saved by rela-
tively simple, low-cost methods. Two and a half million
of them die from dehydration due to diarrhoea, whilst a
solution of eight parts sugar and one part salt in clean
water could save their lives. During his ministry on this
earth, Jesus often took infants up in his arms. Whatever
does he think about the tears of those mothers who are
crying now because there is no hope for their children?

In the next 24 hours more than a thousand young
women will die because of something going wrong at
childbirth. As long as the nutrition of girls is placed second
to that of boys, as long as women eat last and least, and
work hardest and longest, as long as half the babies in the
developing world are delivered with no trained person in
attendance, child-bearing will remain 150 times as dangerous as in the West.

These are just a few of the painful facts brought to
the attention of Christian leaders who attended the 1989
International Congress on World Evangelization in
Manila.[3] They were reminded that vast numbers of those
who hunger and suffer are our fellow Christians. In a

world where 195 million of our brothers and sisters live in absolute poverty, there is surely a particularly relevant message in the story of the twelve baskets. If Jesus did not neglect the destitute, how can we?

The surrendered Christ

Jesus pleases God. In John's account of the feeding of the multitude, he preserves a detail which is not recorded by the other evangelists. At the close of the miraculous meal, certain people in the crowd said, "Surely, this is the Prophet who is to come into the world", and they moved closer to him in order to make him their king. Here was a wonder-working Saviour who would surely rid them of the Roman oppressor. But Jesus knew that this was not his destiny. He would not be king over men's heads until first he was king in their hearts. Jesus got away as quickly as he could. The reading in some older manuscripts says he fled or ran off into the mountains. It may well have been the most dangerous moment in his life. At the beginning of his ministry, the devil offered him all the kingdoms of the world. Jesus deliberately turned away from that kind of kingship at that sort of price. But now, in the guise of applauding admirers, the enemy is, once again, striving to deflect him from his redemptive work.

But, in the moment of subtle temptation, Jesus climbed up into the mountains. He purposely withdrew from the scene where men and women wanted to manipulate him and use him for their purposes rather than God's. By that quick, firm and deliberate action, the Lord Jesus said a resolute "No" to everything less than God's perfect will for his life. Not long before that journey to Bethsaida, he had told his opponents in Jerusalem about what was for him life's greatest ambition: "I seek not to please myself but him who sent me" (5:30). Later, he said the same to some Pharisees who challenged his authority: "I always do what pleases him" (8:29).

Jesus knew that he would wear a crown of thorns before he wore a crown of glory. The path to the throne was by way of a cross, and suffering could not possibly be avoided. The grain of wheat must fall into the ground and die before men would see the promised harvest. Christ devoted himself totally to that predetermined mission of sacrificial service. It cost him his life but it transformed ours.

How Jesus acted on that Galilean hillside left an abiding impression on those two disciples, Andrew and Philip. What those two men said that day was significant, but what they saw was unforgettable. If Jesus was compassionate, why doubt his love? If Christ was sovereign, why question his wisdom? If he was dependent, how foolish for them to be self-reliant. If he was sufficient, why fear the future? If he was sympathetic, how could they possibly dismiss the needs of others? If he was surrendered, then they too must offer their all.

1 William Bridge, *A Lifting Up for the Downcast*, (1648), Banner of Truth Reprint 1961, 32
2 *The State of the World's Children 1989*, Oxford University Press, 40
3 J. D. Douglas, ed., *Proclaim Christ Until He Comes*, published for the Lausanne Committee for World Evangelization, World Wide Publications, Minneapolis, Minnesota 1990, 156

10

DYING TO LIVE

AFTER THE FEEDING of the multitude, another occasion
is described in John's gospel when, once again, Andrew
and Philip appear together. The narrative (12:20–33) con-
tains some of the New Testament's most arresting sayings
about discipleship. We begin by setting the scene for this
important teaching. Although its context is first-century
Jerusalem, it could not possibly be more relevant in late-
twentieth-century Western society.

Jesus and his disciples had gone up to Jerusalem for the
Passover celebrations (12:1–19), arriving early in time to
spend a few days in Bethany to meet up again with Lazarus
who had been raised from the dead. Lazarus' sisters,
Martha and Mary, prepared a meal to welcome Jesus and
it was on this occasion that, out of heartfelt gratitude for
the miracle which had transformed their home, Mary took
a pint of every expensive nard ointment to anoint Jesus as
their honoured guest.

It soon got around that the one who had brought Lazarus dramatically to life was staying in the district. On the
following day, as Jesus left the village, increasing numbers
of people began to join him on his way to the festival. As

he entered Jerusalem, he was publicly acclaimed by a throng of pilgrims who greeted him as Israel's king. They regarded him as the direct fulfilment of Zechariah's prophecy that one day their promised ruler would enter the city riding on a donkey (Zechariah 9:9). In their ascriptions of praise, they quoted a familiar Psalm (118:25), crying out, "Hosanna", which simply means "Save now". They were acknowledging him not only as Zechariah's king but as their Saviour. Significantly enough, those words of the psalmist centuries earlier described one who, though initially rejected like an unwanted stone tossed aside by the builders, would become the chief corner stone, the most prominent and important in the building. Here they were welcoming the promised King, the present Saviour and the despised Stone. When these things were proclaimed in the streets of Jerusalem even the disciples did not fully appreciate the significance of their words (12:16). The people certainly gave public expression to profound truth without realizing what they were saying, a feature found elsewhere in this gospel (11:51).

Talk about the resurrection of Lazarus was spreading quickly amongst the visitors to Jerusalem. Surely someone who could release a corpse from a tomb in Bethany can free a nation from the tyranny of political oppression. If you can raise the dead you are not likely to be hindered by anything. What are a few Roman soldiers to a conqueror of that magnitude? Once again Jesus is in danger of being misunderstood, even by his friends. No wonder that, earlier, on several occasions, he specially asked people not to talk widely about his miraculous acts (Mark 5:43; 7:36). News of that kind could fuel the fires of political unrest. People would argue that, with such a deliverer at hand, why the delay?

But whilst some of the Galilean pilgrims may well have looked to Jesus as a potential liberator, the Jewish authorities viewed him as a dangerous rival. Alarmed about his increasing popularity, and the widening circle of his committed friends (12:17–19), they knew that this couldn't go on: "See, this is getting us nowhere. Look how the whole world has gone after him." It is another example of someone announcing an immense truth without realizing that they are doing it. "The whole world" – that is the theme John is about to explore in the unfolding story.

This, then, is the setting for that special moment when Philip and Andrew sought an interview with Jesus. Some Greek travellers were in Jerusalem for Passover. Possibly they were Greek-speaking Jews, visiting Jerusalem for a major festival, but they may have been devout Gentiles wanting to know more about the Jewish faith, "God-fearers" as they were called. It is interesting that they spoke first to Philip who had grown up in a more Gentile, Greek-speaking culture at Bethsaida. John specially mentions Philip's early life in the town as if that was the point of contact (12:21). Perhaps these Greek pilgrims knew that Philip would understand their outlook and the kind of things they wanted to talk through with his Lord. "We would like to see Jesus", they said to him, and he went off immediately to another Bethsaidan, Andrew, so that together they could bring these enquirers to Jesus.

From a purely human point of view, this reads at first like an almost casual encounter of Passover travellers wanting to meet someone who was very much in the local news. Everybody was talking about what Jesus had done over the past few months. Here was someone who had provided abundant food for a vast crowd of hungry people (6:1–11), walked across the water's surface in the middle of the Sea of Galilee (6:16–21), taught publicly in Jerusalem's Temple (7:14–52), entered into spirited discussion with the religious leaders of his day (8:12–47), angered some of them to the point of fierce hostility (8:59), given sight to a blind man (9:1–41), and raised a dead man to life (11:1–44). Who wouldn't want to see him?

But whatever these Greek visitors made of the interview, Jesus clearly regarded this meeting as one of the most important moments in his life. In this gospel this is the beginning of the end. Alexander Findlay said that Jesus "saw in their coming the rising of the curtain for the final act of the drama". As soon as these Greek visitors were introduced to him he said, "The hour has come for the Son of Man to be glorified." Jesus perceived that the arrival of these seekers was another glimpse of "greater things" (1:50; 5:20; 14:12); his impending sacrifice would usher in a believing response from men and women all over the world. These Greeks were the forerunners of millions of others who would come to the foot of that Cross and put their trust in the one who gave his life for them there.

It is important to see that in the teaching which follows, presumably in the hearing of these enquirers from Greece, Jesus begins to talk about his own forthcoming death. His life is the "grain of wheat" which must fall into the ground and die. If it does, it will produce "many seeds" – like these Greek seekers who were standing there, asking to know more about Jesus. But Christ's initial teaching here about his death also enshrines truths about ours. As we shall see, it then goes on to speak specifically of our death, that "dying to self" which Jesus made such a vital aspect of authentic discipleship: "And anyone who does not carry his cross and follow me cannot be my disciple" (Luke 14:27).

In John 12 Jesus expounds this model of true discipleship in a typically arresting manner, deliberately challenging commonly accepted religious, moral and social values. Like his great prophetic predecessors in the Old Testament, he was compelled to use forceful language and striking imagery in order to get his message across. Jesus presented the truth about his commitment and theirs with the aid of stunning word-pictures, the deliberate shock tactics of Old Testament prophets. People may not like what he says, but they will never be able to forget it: dying is better than living, hating is better than loving, losing is better than keeping, and giving is better than gaining.

Dying is better than living

He was on his way to that Cross, and knew it. The time was limited and the necessity of his death was a stark reality which must be described in compelling, uncompromising phrases. The imagery of the buried seed is simple and familiar, and it will surely fix the message in their minds: "I tell you the truth, unless a grain of wheat falls to the ground and dies, it remains only a single seed. But if it dies, it produces many seeds."

If the solitary seed is left in a storehouse sack, it will retain its identity, but it cannot possibly fulfil its highest purpose. To become what it can be, it must die. It has to be buried, covered, hidden in the darkness; only then can it achieve its staggering potential. To the human eye it will seem lost, gone for ever, but although plunged into the cold earth, it will slowly begin to release its life.

The context of this saying of Jesus heightens its significance. It is uttered in the setting of inevitable death. To the outsider everything around seemed to be throbbing with eager life. The meal table at Bethany had been surrounded with grateful guests, the crowds had pressed around Jesus as he walked to the city, admiring followers lifted him on to a donkey, Galilean pilgrims acclaimed him as their deliverer. Hosannahs were ringing in the air; it was a time of rejoicing. Israel's king had come.

But things were not quite as they appeared. In that village home the previous night, Mary had broken open a jar of costly ointment which the sisters had stored away for a long time. In Jewish households, treasure of that kind was kept by for anointing a body before burial. It was a family's way of expressing, for the last time, adoring love for someone who would be greatly missed. Judas complained that to use it to anoint a guest's feet was a gross waste of money. He spluttered something about the needs of the poor, but few people were listening. Everybody's eyes were on Jesus. He spoke quietly in defence of the woman, saying something that everybody remembered because it took them so completely by surprise: "It was intended that she should save this perfume for the day of my burial . . . you will not always have me." In a setting of life, he talked about death.

Lazarus was there when his sister, kneeling at the feet of Jesus, used her hair as a towel. Everything looked fine for Lazarus. Miraculously, death was a thing of the past. But it was not really so. So persuasive was Lazarus' testimony to the power and uniqueness of Christ that he too was becoming spiritually influential, like his Master: "on account of him many of the Jews were going over to Jesus and putting their faith in him". The priests made sure that the name of Lazarus was on their hit-list alongside that of Jesus. Death for him might be alarmingly near.

In her loving welcome, a believing woman anticipated his death. Now her brother was identifying with his death: "So the chief priests made plans to kill Lazarus as well." Even the joyous festival which brought the pilgrims together had a message about sacrifice. It was Passover time and, although a season of grateful celebration, death was at the heart of that story too. Lambs had to be slain; dying was inevitable.

It was in this menacing setting that Jesus talked about his own death. Others are born to live; he came specially to die. If he did not die then others would not live. If that unique life remained "a single seed" there could have been no salvation. If he had deliberately clung to his life, the chief priests and scribes might not have been able to arrest him. He told his captors that an army of angels could easily rescue him (Matthew 26:53). But, if they had, he would not have fulfilled his divinely-appointed mission, and we would have been left with the "single seed" of his superlative life. If, supernaturally, Jesus had been delivered from that awful death, only the solitary seed would have remained: the "single seed" of a beautiful life which people could always admire but that is all. It would have been a story of matchless example but, in the end, little more than a painful embarrassment – exalting all he most certainly was, and pointedly exposing what we are not. The "single seed" would have left us with his incomparable teaching but, without his indwelling power, it would have remained as unattainable idealism. His pure and spotless life alone would have revealed us as we are, unclean sinners with no hope of changing ourselves.

But the seed died, as Jesus said it must. At the anointing, Mary prefigured the inevitability of his death. Lazarus illustrated the malignity of his death. It was cruelly vindictive to hunt Lazarus down. The Passover lambs typified the guiltlessness of his death, and those Greek seekers anticipated the effect of his death. The one dying seed was the first of "many seeds". Already, as Jesus talked about it, people were coming, like these Greeks, from another nation, and a different culture. To recall the imagery of his earlier teaching, here, in embryo, were the "other sheep" of a distant fold (10:15–16), and the Shepherd was ready to lay down his life for them.

But in this passage the Saviour's dying is a pattern for the disciple's living. Once, when he was home on furlough, James Calvert, the nineteenth-century Wesleyan missionary to the cannibals of Fiji, was asked by a fearful inquirer, "Were you not afraid of being killed ?" "No", Calvert replied, "we died before we went."[1] That is the secret. Those who follow Jesus know that they must surrender the selfish life. They are ready to die to all those things in life which may not please him. Moreover, it is not a "once for all" experience. They die each day to everything contrary to his teaching, anything alien to his example. Their unbelieving contemporaries, determined to squeeze every drop out of "life" for themselves, are baffled by this willing Christian renunciation. But disciples know from the example of Jesus, the teaching of Scripture, and the story of faith across the centuries that "dying" is always better than "living". They have proved that those who truly die are the only ones who really live.

Hating is better than loving

Yet, someone will say, surely all this is contrary to our human nature. It is natural to love ourselves, satisfy ourselves, even exalt ourselves. But Jesus says that will not do. His disciples put God's will, Christ's example and the Spirit's message before their self-centred desires. It will mean deliberately assigning our personal wishes to second place, but such a resolute decision will not only mean a more fulfilled life here, but a more useful one, to say nothing of a secure one in eternity. It means "hating" ourselves, said Jesus, which was vivid Hebrew idiom for "loving less". It is the uncompromising language of essential choice. Jesus put it starkly so that all his disciples would always remember: "The man who loves his life will lose it, while the man who hates his life in this world will keep it for eternal life."

The alternatives are presented with unmistakable clarity – greedily clutching our claim on this life will cause us to lose the best in it; pleasing ourselves in this world may mean forfeiting the next. What Jesus is saying with piercing forcefulness is that if we really want to enjoy this life we must enjoy him far more. The secret is in loving him more than all others. The late-medieval spiritual writer, Walter Hilton, put it searchingly: "If you want to know what it is you love, just consider what it is you are *usually* thinking about." Going about his daily work in a fourteenth-century Midlands community, Hilton was usually thinking about Jesus, next about his fellow believers, and rarely about himself. That is what hating ourselves means, and we must certainly be loved much less by ourselves if we are ever to be the kind of disciples he can use. Disciples constantly move away from the centre of the stage. The most prominent position is reserved for him.

What effect is this likely to have in our everyday lives? If Jesus always comes first, that will often be costly. It will frequently cut directly across our natural inclinations. This is surely what Jesus meant when he talked about "cutting off our right hand" or "throwing away our right eye" (Matthew 5:27–30) if our Christian development is at stake. It is intentionally harsh metaphorical language, recognizing the price of obedience to him.

We all know those areas of our personal life and thought where we are morally vulnerable and spiritually weak. "Hating ourselves" means we keep well away from the arena of specific temptation. For example, it is spiritually irresponsible to read something or look at things which might create or stimulate unhelpful visual images or lower our spiritual resistance. There is a mental pornography which needs to be handled as ruthlessly as the printed kind. The vivid imagery of removing the eye or hand is meant to emphasize that all this is nothing if it is not costly. Holiness is never cheap. But it is better by far to be considered out of fashion or prudishly unliberated because you have not read this or that new book, seen that film or TV programme, then end up less than the person whom you genuinely long to be. Being socially "maimed" is a small price to pay for that kind of purity which pleases God, helps others and improves us.

The same emphasis on self-renunciation is found elsewhere in the New Testament. When Paul is teaching the Christians at Rome about radical Christian living he emphasizes the necessity of "putting to death the misdeeds of the body" so that, in the power of the Spirit, we can really "live" (Romans 8:13). He explains that men and women have a sinful nature which in turn produces sinful thoughts which actively plan sinful deeds (Romans 8:4, 5, 13). But those believers who have given themselves entirely to Christ and have placed themselves under the Holy Spirit's control are determined "not to live according to the sinful nature" (8:4). Their minds are not "set on what that nature desires". They have higher ambitions by far. Their minds concentrate "on what the Spirit desires" (8:5) which means that evil thoughts and longings are slain within them long before those natural inclinations become damaging acts – and all this is achieved by the dynamic ministry of the indwelling Holy Spirit.

Losing is better than keeping

The events at Bethany have provided an illustration of these striking opposites. With adoring love, Mary pours the costly perfume over the feet of Jesus, but Judas is doing his sums. His cold, calculating mind is working out how ridiculously expensive this bit of over-generous hospitality really is. Mary is passionately concerned about what she can give. Judas is frighteningly preoccupied with what he can get. The loving woman's secret question is, "What may I give him?" The heartless man's enquiry is, "What will you give me?" When Matthew relates his account of a meal-table anointing, he consciously sets the two stories side by side. It seems as if he specially wants us to see Mary and Judas as contrasting personalities. The commendation of the Master is followed by the condemnation of the traitor: "She did it to prepare me for burial . . . Then . . . Judas Iscariot went to the chief priests and asked, 'What are you willing to give me if I hand him over to you?'" (Matthew 26:6–16). The woman has spilt the ointment, and within minutes, Judas is rushing to collect his money. He would have liked the cost of the perfume, but he can at least have the cost of the Redeemer.

But by parting with her treasure, Mary has lost nothing.

Indeed, she has gained everything. By clutching his money Judas has lost everything. Those silver coins, once so important to him, are suddenly valueless. Too late, he has seen what really matters in life. Agonized, he hurls his money down those same Temple steps which, hours before, he had hurriedly climbed to collect his precious silver. He has lost not just his money, but his life and his destiny.

In a variety of different ways this gospel makes it abundantly clear that material things never bring lasting satisfaction (4:32–34; 6:27; 12:4–8). Our enjoyment of them does not even extend to this life, let alone that which is to come. A famous West End actor and film star died a few months ago at the age of 87. One of his obituary notices included his sad personal confession:

"My trouble is that I was always very materialistic. I owned 12 horses, 7 Rolls Royces. I've had mistresses in Paris, London and New York, and it never made me happy."

Giving is better than gaining

Jesus says to these Greek enquirers, Andrew, Philip and others who may have been standing nearby, "Whoever serves me must follow me" and that means following him to the place of total surrender: "Where I am, my servant also will be" (John 12:26). And where will Jesus be? At the Cross.

At that precise moment, in the street in Jerusalem, Jesus experiences a sudden anticipation of Gethsemane's testing. It is as if he specially wants his disciples to realize that "hating" life at this point or that is not easy. Even Jesus was deeply disturbed when the time of sacrifice drew near. The Son knew how costly it was at this point to let the grain of wheat fall into the ground and die: "Now my heart is troubled, and what shall I say? 'Father, save me from this hour?' No, it was for this very reason I came to this hour. Father, glorify your name!"

Jesus knew that only as he was "lifted up from the earth" at Calvary would people like his eager disciples, Andrew and Philip, and those enquiring Greeks be drawn to him (12:32). He knew the severe cost, but he had entered the world with an unflinching resolution to do the Father's will and glorify the Father's name (6:38; 17:1; Hebrews 10:5–9). That is why, when Jesus offered the sacrificial prayer "Glorify your name!", the Father replied so quickly:

"Then a voice came from heaven, 'I have glorified it, and will glorify it again.' "

Some people thought that the sound they heard was the rumbling of distant thunder. There will always be those who in moments of crisis are strangely deaf to the voice of God. Others, a little more attuned to spiritual reality, said the noise may have been the whisper of a supporting angel. But it was the Father who was speaking, as he had at his Son's baptism when he committed himself publicly to the Father's will, and at his Transfiguration, when he was acclaimed before men as God's obedient Son (Matthew 3:17; 17:5).

As he stood in the shadow of inevitable death, Jesus was giving himself afresh to the Father. In the public street as Christ had spoken, people were standing all around, very different people. There were disciples who longed to follow him, whatever the cost, Greeks who genuinely wanted to know what following meant, and casual bystanders who could only attend to outward things like audible sounds, rarely to the quiet voice of inner pleading. But the Father was glorified in the renewed surrender of his obedient Son, and he would be glorified again both at the Cross, and whenever his disciples were willing to follow him there.

Jesus knew that by giving his life, there would be infinite gain, and the increase could not be achieved in any other way. The seed must die if there was to be an abundant harvest. That death of Christ was unique, of course. By that saving sacrifice alone, men and women are cleansed, forgiven, redeemed and changed. But it also provides a pattern for genuine discipleship. Peter had it right when he wrote about it not only as a substitutionary death for our salvation but as a perfect example for our sanctification. He said that to people who were slaves, social nobodies in the first-century Roman empire, some of them suffering, even severely, for their faith. "You must make Jesus your model", he said to them: "Christ suffered for you, leaving you an example, that you should follow in his steps" (1 Peter 2:21). That word "example" is the term commonly used in the first-century world to describe the large letters which a teacher wrote at the top of a slate so that the young pupil could copy them, and thus make the perfectly formed letters of the alphabet. Jesus is the perfect pattern of a surrendered life. By giving all, he gained everything for us. Disciples follow him to the place of total self-giving.

But we must not think of that surrender solely as something excruciatingly painful. We will not make the sacrifice in our own strength and, let us remember, we will never make it to our own detriment. Jesus told his men that if they gave up anything for him in this life, they would receive far more in return (Luke 18:18–30). But when they let the seed die, they have to trust him that there will be a harvest. It is an act of daring faith. The harvest is not visible when the seed dies.

At the 1989 International Congress on World Evangelization at Manila, Archbishop David Penman told the story of a Christian salesman who had been away from home for several days at a regional conference. The closing session had over-run its time and, as soon as it was over, he hurried with his friends to the main-line station. They had barely enough time to catch a train which would get them back early enough to spend some of the evening with their families. If they missed that particular train, there would be a considerable wait before the next, and they would be very late home.

As the group charged through the terminal, the Christian man inadvertently kicked over a small table supporting a vendor's box of fruit. Apples tumbled out and rolled across the floor in all directions, but the men rushed on to the platform with only seconds to spare before the train left. As they boarded the train, the man responsible for the accident stopped in his tracks, almost unable to move. His colleagues urged him to catch the train but, deep inside, he felt desperately unhappy. Should he go on or go back? He had noticed a young boy, about ten years old, standing by the table, selling the apples. In those few seconds, before the train pulled out, one question suddenly took control of his mind: What would Jesus do now?

More than anything, he longed to be back with his family but, in that moment, following Christ became more important than getting home. Waving goodbye to his puzzled friends, he briskly made his way back to the main concourse. People were rushing for their trains, dodging the apples. Many had been kicked here and there by hurrying travellers and the Christian man was puzzled that the lad had done nothing whatever to retrieve his apples. As he got closer, he realized why the boy was just standing there, dazed and helpless. He was blind.

Quickly the salesman began to collect the apples. Setting up the table again, he could see that many of them were badly bruised. Opening his wallet, he took out a note, pressed it into the boy's hand, saying, "Here, please take this ten dollars for the damage we did. Hope we haven't spoilt your day." Slowly he began to walk away when, above the noise in the station, he heard the loud voice of the boy calling after him, "Sir, are you Jesus?"

Now he knew why he had been meant to stay. Had he pleased himself, he would certainly have caught the train. But the boy would have been left on the station, alone in the dark, pained and bewildered. But in that second on the platform, facing the slowly-moving train, he met the challenge to lose his life rather than love it. Just then, it meant deliberately hating what he really liked doing. It was a renewed call to follow in the steps of Jesus: "Where I am, my servant also will be." For a moment, it was costly, but he had received an immense reward. He had not simply met a blind boy's need. He had overheard the most wonderful tribute in the world.

When the Greeks came seeking Jesus, they eventually saw him *with* his disciples. Nowadays, they need to see him *in* his disciples. That theme takes us to our closing chapter.

1 Joseph Nettleton, *John Hunt*, London undated, 27

11

SHOW US THE FATHER

WE HAVE COME NOW to an occasion in John's Gospel when one of our three disciples makes a special request to Jesus. Christ's reply to that request (14:8–13) provides us with some key teaching about discipleship in the modern world. Here Jesus shares with his friend Philip some of his priorities for living, and makes it clear that they need to be ours too.

In our previous chapter we looked at the response of the Lord Jesus to the quest of the enquiring Greeks (12:20–33). From chapter 13 onwards, the reader of this Gospel is acutely aware of a different environment or context for its message. Up to and including chapter 12, we have been in the presence of Jesus as he mainly confronts the hostile or apathetic world. We had been warned in the Prologue that this would be so. Some might reject the light and choose the darkness. In the unbelieving world he was neither identified nor welcomed: "the world did not recognize him" and "his own did not receive him" (1:10–11). Yet to this kind of unresponsive audience he had, with strenuous zeal and incomparable skill, used every opportunity to convey his message by means of verbal and visible truth, word and sign.

The verbal communication was by superb teaching with the aid of arresting images and unforgettable pictures – the rebuilt Temple, the new birth, the indwelling spring of life-giving water, bread which banished hunger for ever, a fountain to quench all thirst, light so permanent that people never walk in the darkness again, the shepherd who surrenders his life for the sheep (2:19; 3:3; 4:14; 6:35; 7:37; 8:12; 10:11).

And, added to that creative use of illustration, there was the skill to interpret afresh some of the magnificent stories and sayings of the Old Testament, so familiar to most of the people he longed to reach: Jacob's open heaven (1:51), David's consuming zeal (2:17), Moses' uplifted serpent (3:14), the Israelites' manna in the desert (6:30–33), Isaiah's never-failing spring (7:38–39; Isaiah 58:11), and Ezekiel's one shepherd (10:16; Ezekiel 34:23; 37:24).

But the truth had to be communicated visually as well as verbally. Jesus knew that word alone would not convince them. In Old Testament times, when God spoke things happened. His words did not simply describe his power; they conveyed it. He had only to say something must happen, and it was done. So, that same "power through the word" had to be manifest in his Son if the hesitant were to be turned from caution to commitment. Therefore, all his miracles are found in this opening section with the exception of the astonishing catch of fish, purposely withheld until his brilliant Epilogue. These "signs" (as John prefers to call them) were intended as "teaching in action". They were visible demonstrations of his deity.

John describes in detail these merciful interventions in

human life – a happy wedding-celebration in Cana, a healed boy in Capernaum, a transformed paralytic in Jerusalem, a hunger-relieved crowd at Bethsaida, a stilled storm on Galilee, a grateful beggar whose blindness was washed away at Siloam's Pool, and a man from Bethany, newly-liberated from his own tomb. Surely God, in Christ, has spoken his transforming word. Yet, in spite of all this, we are still in the company of deliberate Christ-rejectors. Neither word or sign convince them of anything. By the time we reach the close of chapter 12, Christ is being ruthlessly pursued: "So from that day on they plotted to take his life" (11:53). Those who follow him are in equal danger (12:10–11), and the cost of commitment has caused many true disciples to keep their allegiance a secret. Fear sealed their lips, and exposed, sadly, their preference of human praise to divine approval (12:42–43).

All this is dramatic backcloth for the changed context from chapter 13 onwards. The more public ministry is over. The scene has moved from the Temple courts to the Upper Room. Now, we are in the company of committed but bewildered believers. The immediate need is not further signs, but sustaining words. In these chapters the message of Jesus emerges initially by means of a series of questions or comments made by five of the disciples. At Peter's request, John asks about the identity of the betrayer (13:24–25). Peter then enquires about the immediate intentions of Jesus (13:36). Thomas wants to know the way to the place where Jesus plans to go (14:5). Philip longs for a revelation of the Father (14:8), and Judas (not Iscariot) wants to know why the promised manifestation of Christ's glory is exclusively for the disciples (14:22). We all learn by asking questions. Philip's request for further light, and how Jesus replied, is important for our understanding of discipleship.

What Jesus says to Philip and the others in this upper room is that his own relationship with the Father is a model for their relationship with Him. He has been telling them that if they want to know what the Father is like, they have only to look at their Lord. If they really knew Jesus as God's Son and the perfect revelation of his Father, then they would know God too. Jesus tells them that as they have been watching him, they have been looking into the face of their heavenly Father. Jesus says of his Father: "From now on you do know him and have seen him" (14:7).

Still Philip does not understand. He imagines that in this time of threatening uncertainty and crisis, they would all be sustained by a special, extra revelation of their Father God: "Lord, show us the Father." If they were to pass through hard times, could Jesus not ensure that they might have a spectacular enabling vision of God's glory as, say, Abraham (Genesis 17:1–22), or Moses (Exodus 33:18–23), or Joshua (5:13–15), or Isaiah (6:1–8), or Ezekiel (1:1–28), or Daniel (7:9–14) had, to strengthen and equip them for the difficult times which seemed to lie ahead.

Jesus makes the point that they need no further theophany. They have been looking into God's face all through the past three years of Christ's ministry: "Anyone who has seen me has seen the Father." But, although Christ had often told them that he was one with the Father, and dependent on him for everything, words and deeds, yet Philip for one had not grasped that essential truth. Perhaps he was ignorant of it: "Don't you *know* me, Philip, even after I have been with you for such a long time?" Perhaps he was uncommitted to it: "Don't you *believe* that I am in the Father, and that the Father is in me?" Possibly, like so many of us, Philip had heard the truth in the top of his mind, but he had not accepted it in the bottom of his heart.

Jesus used this moment to share some profound truths with his disciples about his priorities and theirs. Throughout his ministry, he had been supported by the inseparable union he had enjoyed with his Father and, if they were to be remotely effective in such a hostile world, the relationship he had with God must become a pattern for their commitment to him. It had five characteristics and each one is as significant for modern disciples as it was for Philip and his friends. In his unhindered relationship with God, Jesus had revealed his Father's nature, shared his Father's words, done his Father's works, needed his Father's help, and sought his Father's glory. We too must express our commitment by what we are, say, do, need and want.

Showing the Father's nature

Jesus is mildly astonished that Philip had not properly grasped this basic fact about his Incarnation and subsequent life and ministry. He was in the world to show what God is like. The Old Testament portraiture of God was reliable but fragmentary, inspiring but partial. As God's unique Son, Jesus came so that men and women need never be in doubt about God's nature – righteous but merciful, loving but strong, holy but patient. In this encounter, Philip starkly illustrates the point that we can hear truth without believing it, and know truth without appropriating it.

Those words of Jesus addressed to his disciple should pierce our hearts as well: "Don't you know?" and "Don't you believe?" We need to ask ourselves what we are doing practically to become better informed about our faith. Do we read God's Word every day and do we determine not to rise from that daily exercise until we have grasped afresh one striking truth and strenuously endeavoured to apply that message to our own everyday lives? Do we meet at one time or another with a group of fellow-believers either at work, home, or church, where our fellow members are zealous for Christian truth and passionate about relating it to life in contemporary society? Have we appreciated the value of good Christian books, or well-produced educative videos, as excellent tools to equip us with the message of God's ever-relevant Word? Is Jesus saying to us: 'Don't you *know* . . . ?'

Or have we allowed great biblical doctrines to wash over our minds without accepting them deeply for ourselves? Are they just massive theological themes but belonging to distant worlds, truths we have not begun to accept at any deep level? What are we doing to get them from our head to our heart? Is Jesus saying to us: "Don't you *believe*?" That does not simply mean intellectual acceptance; it demands wholehearted commitment. In his *Saints' Everlasting Rest*, Richard Baxter shared his spiritual "ten directions" with his seventeenth-century contemporaries. They included this plea:

"Let all your knowledge turn into affection and practice; keep open the passage between your heads and your hearts, that every truth may go to the quick."

In other words, make sure you apply biblical truth to life in the contemporary world. If we accept the biblical doctrine of God's loving nature, then we cannot condone severed relationships with others, even when it is not easy to love (Matthew 5:43–48). If we are persuaded about God's providential care, then we must stop worrying (Matthew 6:25–34). If we recognize God's holy character, then we must be holy too (1 Peter 1:15–16).

Philip and his partners came to see that the Christ who had manifested the Father *to* them was wanting to reveal the Father *through* them. After he left them, they were to live as his believing children in the world, reflecting their Father's character, cherishing his ideals, maintaining his standards, pursuing his will: "If anyone loves me he will obey my teaching. My Father will love him, and we will come to him and make our home with him" (14:23). Moreover, this ambition was not only what Jesus taught to them but prayed for them in this gospel: "I have made you known to them, and will continue to make you known in order that the love you have for me may be in them and that I myself may be in them" (17:26).

Therefore this teaching about discipleship emphasizes that those who are committed to Christ will share the Son's ambition. It will be their greatest desire to live in such a way that the Father's qualities are revealed in their daily lives. Christ's revelation of the Father was obviously unique because he was totally sinless, but we must never use our imperfect nature as an excuse for lower ideals. If Jesus said we are to be merciful as our Father in heaven is merciful (Luke 6:36), then it must be attainable. He would never command us to do the impossible. Therefore, modern disciples are to reveal the Father's characteristics by what they are; the truth must be visible in their lives.

Sharing the Father's words

Jesus does not only reveal the Father by his life style; he shares God's words as well. His message is truth he has received directly from his Father. He had not come into the world as an independent and innovative communicator. He said that to Philip in terms the disciple could not possibly misunderstand: "The words I say to you are not just my own." Moreover, Jesus says the same thing repeatedly on other occasions as well (7:16; 8:28; 12:49–50; 14:24). He knows that although he embodies the truth in his person, men and women will still need to hear it from his lips.

What is evident is not always obvious without verbal explanation. For example, that assurance which Jesus had given to Philip about his unique deity had to be communicated by words if it was to be understood and believed. The disciple could not have been expected to grasp it fully without it being given in aural form: "I am in the Father and the Father is in me. The words I say to you are not just my own." The word about his deity confirmed the reality of his deity. Had Jesus not said it no Jew would dream of believing it. It was, after all, that affirmation of his unique relationship with the Father which made his contemporaries label him as a blasphemer. It was an appalling offence for any Jew to claim equality with God. Yet, flying in the face of conventional teaching, his disciples dared to accept the word of Jesus. The word was vital if the message was to be believed.

So, if disciples are to follow (12:26) in the steps of their Master, they too must communicate the Word. Jesus received the Word from the Father and faithfully transmitted it to his disciples. They too must take that Word and accurately convey it to their contemporaries. Learners are to enlist more learners, and that can only be done by passing on the Word. The revelation of Christ's uniqueness is not a truth to be secretly hoarded but widely shared. In every century true disciples have been eager to make other disciples.

It was an unbelievably happy day for Thomas Bilney when God's truth leapt from the pages of the New Testament and showed him beyond doubt that Christ had died for his sins. That sixteenth-century Cambridge friar had bought a copy of Erasmus's translation of the New Testament, more "allured by the Latin than by the word of God":

> But at last I heard speak of Jesus . . . and at the first reading (as I well remember) I chanced upon this sentence of St Paul (O most sweet and comfortable sentence to my soul!) in 1 Timothy 1: "It is a true saying, and worthy of all men to be embraced, that Christ Jesus came into the world to save sinners, of whom I am the chief and principal." This one sentence, through God's instruction and inward working, which I did not then perceive, did so exhilarate my heart, being before wounded with the guilt of my sins, and being almost in despair, that immediately I felt a marvellous comfort and quietness, insomuch that my bruised bones leaped for joy.[1]

But, overwhelming gratitude for his new-found faith made him not merely exhilarated but eloquent. The indebted disciple had to find someone with whom he could share his joy. Bilney aimed high. He sought an opportunity to talk with another Cambridge man, the most famous preacher of his day, Hugh Latimer. But how could he begin to share his testimony effectively with someone who at that time was so fiercely opposed to the Reformation message? "Little Bilney" as he was affectionately known, quietly asked Latimer if he could confess his soul to him. The preacher naturally thought Bilney wanted to confess his sins; in reality he wanted to confess his Saviour. The bold witness was used to bring Latimer to an equally convinced and robust faith. In God's mercy, one disciple had won another. The converted Latimer was to preach the Gospel with compelling fluency until the day when, like Bilney, he also went to the stake, dying for the faith he lived by.

Those men shared the truth at great cost. Mercifully, in our day, martyrdom is rare. But if that is so, we must not fail to grasp the opportunities which come our way to share our faith with others. The Lord longs to use us in this ministry of personal witnessing and, for that reason, he will create the openings for us. It will not be necessary for us artificially to manoeuvre conversation until we can tortuously steer it round to a spiritual topic. At the right time, people around us will make comments or ask questions or issue challenges which only a coward could avoid. In preparation for those God-given occasions, we need to pray that we will keep on being filled (which is what Paul means in Ephesians 5:18) with the Holy Spirit who alone can equip us with the words and the love (Romans 5:5) we need in evangelism. But speak we must, for the Father's love will become evident in what we say as well as by what we are.

Doing the Father's works

Yet, words alone may not convince the unbeliever. Despite his faithful teaching, those who did not acknowledge Christ were still looking for irrefutable proof of his power. They still are. But just as God had spoken to him so he had worked through him. Jesus made it clear to Philip that it was the Father who had made possible the remarkable signs which had accompanied his preaching. Words and works were inseparable: "The *words* I say to you are not just my own. Rather, it is the Father, living in me, who is doing his *work*." Jesus recognized that some would not be able to accept the assertion about his deity solely on the basis of what he said. Something visible, as well as verbal, would have to authenticate the claim. Patient as he always was, Jesus understood that, and this is how he put it to Philip: "Believe me when I *say* that I am in the Father and the Father is in me; or at least believe on the evidence of the *miracles* themselves."

All through John's gospel the people were asking for signs to confirm that Jesus was all he claimed to be (2:18; 4:48; 6:30). Yet, this gospel makes it equally plain that, however many signs he performed, most of his contemporaries were resolutely determined not to believe in him (12:37). The signs themselves would not convince them that he was the matchless Son of God. He could restore the dying, heal the cripple, feed the hungry, tread the waves, illuminate the blind, raise the dead, or anything else, and they still would not put their faith in him (Matthew 11:20–24; 12:38–42; Mark 8:11–12).

It was not only unbelievers who were not persuaded on the basis of Christ's miraculous works. Even an outstandingly godly man like John the Baptist did not find them convincing enough to rob him of his deep uncertainties in Herod's dungeon: "When John heard in prison what Jesus was doing, he sent his disciples to ask him, 'Are you the one who was to come, or should we expect someone else?' " (Matthew 11:3). News of great miracles did little to silence his doubts in that dark prison at Machaerus on the eastern side of the Dead Sea.

If he was ever permitted to look out from that fortress, John might even have seen in the distance the very place where he had baptized people by their hundreds and called them urgently to repentance in the light of the coming wrath. John could recall vividly the warnings he had issued and the plea he had made. Why was the threatened judgment delayed?

Jesus told the messengers to return with a message not simply about what they had *seen* but about what God had *said*. By his signs Jesus was fulfilling all that was predicted of him in Isaiah's prophecy centuries before (Isaiah 35:4–6). Then, Jesus added a warm, encouraging word to the pained doubter: "Blessed is the man who does not fall away on account of me" (Matthew 11:6). Happy are the believers who are not stumbled because I am not working in precisely the way they expect. John had his own notion as to how the Messiah ought to be dealing with unbelieving people. It was time the winnowing fork was in his hand. The axe of judgment should not be laid to the roots of proud trees – those arrogant, immoral opponents like Herod and his henchmen. But Jesus was working as God wanted him to at that moment of time. Those were days for different "works" than those which John expected. John heard a lot about the miracles of Jesus but he still wondered whether the Christ had really come. However spectacular the signs they do not automatically create or encourage faith.

All this is exceptionally important in the current "Signs and Wonders" debate. Nobody who takes the Bible seriously wishes to doubt for a moment God's power to heal. Thousands of believing people throughout the world can personally testify to the fact that he can and does. But "Power Evangelism", to use the popular phrase, suggests that if our contemporaries saw these New Testament miracles like curing the cripples and healing the deaf taking place in our own times, then they would find it impossible not to believe in Christ. But that is not necessarily so. To say that would be to assert that modern miracles would be more persuasive than Christ's. His did not convert all his contemporaries from stubborn unbelief to radiant faith. Even those who wanted to believe, like John the Baptist, were not totally persuaded by miracles.

Moreover, even if a miracle takes place in our own day, it is by no means self-evident to our contemporaries that it is the work of Jesus. In the first instance, our unbelieving neighbours will begin by explaining it away by natural means. Additionally, if they are wise and biblically literate, Christian believers will not automatically assume that every "miracle" is the Lord's doing. We too would have to admit that not all events which might be described as miraculous acts are God-inspired. Egypt had her miracle-workers in Moses' day. They did remarkable things (Exodus 7:10–11, 20–22; 8:6–7) and God's Word does nothing to conceal it. Sinister forces can be at work in our world as much as theirs, causing changes and transformations in natural life which are not easily explained by scientific means. Missionaries who have served in Third World countries have witnessed sinister things happening, humanly inexplicable, but they are not "miracles" which the Lord would either inspire or honour. In twentieth-century Western society people have been "healed" through the work of mediums in Spiritualist seances. Does that mean that such "signs" are of God?

Even Christ's uniquely compassionate signs were not immediately successful in convincing either his unbelieving contemporaries or hesitant doubters. Why, then, does Jesus make this astonishing promise to Philip that, in the future, he and his colleagues would witness signs even more spectacular? What could be more authenticating than raising the dead? Did Jesus really mean that their forthcoming "works" would be more impressive than his own? It sounds remarkably like that: "I tell you the truth, anyone who has faith in me will do what I have been doing. He will do even greater things than these, because I am going to the Father." This dramatic saying certainly needs explanation and we must now think carefully about its message for modern disciples. Three things need to be said: These "greater things" that are promised cannot be greater in quality, they will be greater in extent, and they must be greater in character.

The "greater things" promised by Jesus to his disciples cannot be greater in quality. It is impossible to believe that he was really saying that what happened at Bethany's tomb would later be dwarfed by more sensational miracles at the hands of the disciples. Even those who want to insist that Jesus is here referring essentially to repeated physical miracles of healing have to admit that resurrections are rare in the contemporary world. And what a mercy they are. Christ (not the devil) has the keys of Death and Hades, he said to John on Patmos. That word of assurance (Revelation 1:17–18) was spoken to a man and his believing contemporaries who were living under the threat of arrest and execution by the imperial magistrates. The exalted Christ was telling John that nobody will die in Christ until the moment when Jesus decides that it is meant to be. If, in his Lordship of the next world as well as this (Romans 14:7–9), he has determined that a believer's work on earth is over, what right have we to want to bring that person back?

Jesus can hardly be saying that his disciples would be working miracles more spectacular than those which characterized Christ's ministry on earth. Are his followers in the modern world expected to look for something more convincing than transforming water into wine, more memorable than walking on the sea, more impressive than giving sight to a man with congenital blindness? Certainly we must not say that these things cannot happen. God will work in his world however he wishes, but we are surely meant to ask whether miracles more dazzling than these are the "greater things" Jesus was talking about.

They cannot be greater in quality, but they will be greater in extent – geographically, culturally, and numerically. The whole of Christ's ministry was largely confined geographically to the narrow limits of his own very small country. He visited the coastal towns of Phoenicia (Matthew 15:21) and the cities of the Decapolis (Mark 5:1; 7:31), just beyond Israel's border, but that was all. But the "greater things" promised by Jesus would take place all over the known world just beyond his earthly life-time. Dedicated heralds would proclaim his truth in countries Jesus had never visited. Paul would expound the riches of Christ from Jerusalem all the way across Asia Minor, over into Europe, through Greece and up to Yugoslavia. His feet would walk the streets of Rome and he would dream of reaching Spain. That was a "greater thing" geographically than even Jesus had known.

It was "greater" culturally too. Christ spoke in one language and spelt out the truth to his contemporaries in his native tongue, but within weeks of his ascension, Jerusalem would be packed with visitors from all over the Mediterranean world. They were there for the festival of Pentecost and, by the unique miracle of the Holy Spirit's working, a "greater thing" happened in those Jerusalem streets than any Hebrew or Aramaic speaker had ever said or heard. Everybody heard the wonders of God's deeds in their own tongue, and thousands came to personal faith. It was a faith which transcended barriers. They proclaimed a truth which bridged the huge gulfs of the first-century world – the social gulf which isolated freemen from slaves, the religious gulf which separated Jews and Gentiles, the sexual gulf which exalted men above women. Even the political gulf was overcome, that between conformists and revolutionaries. Matthew, the pro-Roman tax collector and Simon the anti-Roman zealot had sat side by side at the Lord's Table, and they were forerunners of many thousands of others who, throughout history, would be reconciled in Christ. Harsh and violent antagonisms would be banished. Jesus had ushered in a "greater thing" than ever his earliest followers would have believed.

Those new things the disciples could expect would be numerically "greater", of course. The Saviour had gathered around him a team of twelve men, a small group of ministering women, a wider circle of responsive believers but, after three years' hard work, only one hundred and twenty gathered in Jerusalem to seek the power for the new task. But, by Pentecost the numbers began to escalate. "Greater things" were happening because Jesus had ascended. He had told them that his heavenly exaltation must take place first, because only then would the Holy Spirit be given, and without the Spirit "greater things" are never possible.

At Pentecost the Spirit came in a way he had never visited people before, as Jesus said he would, and soon the modest group were quickly joined by thousands more. Throughout the decades and centuries which followed people have come to trust in Jesus by their millions, and now, in the late twentieth century, the numbers are greater still. It is estimated that of the world's 5.2 billion people, one-third call themselves Christians, and about half of these are believers in faith and practice. About 14,000 people are said to be brought to Christ daily. There are one and a half million churches or congregations scattered throughout the world. Just over 1,500 new local churches are started every day. There are just about the same number of radio and television programmes with almost a million listeners every month.[2] It is not exactly a failure-story! These are certainly "greater things" than anything which could have happened during the brief span of Jesus' ministry on earth.

But they will not only be greater in extent. They must also be greater in character. Christ's miracles were, for the greater part, dramatic, public and immediate healings. But even those who were changed physically, still had to face eternity without him, unless they were spiritually trans-formed as well. The priority of spiritual healing over physi-cal transformation was demonstrated by Jesus for all time when he gave strength to the paralytic in Capernaum, the man brought by his friends to Jesus, and dramatically lowered through a hole in the roof (Mark 2:1–12). Jesus began by pardoning his sins: "Son, your sins are forgiven".

That was the man's greater need. His authority to do such a thing was challenged by his opponents but, to demonstrate the power of his Word, Jesus went on to give immediate strength to the man's paralysed limbs. The man responded immediately, walking out in full view of everyone, carping critics as well as thankful friends. The Word which had imparted life was the same Word which had guaranteed cleansing. No rational person could doubt either his right or his power to forgive and change sinners.

That, surely, is the "greater thing" which Jesus would do through his disciples in the future. It was not that the disciples' works would transcend his. New miracles would still be wrought by Christ, but through his disciples in the power of the Spirit, and still for the glory of God. However earnest their prayers and however rich their faith, blind people might not necessarily receive their sight again, but they would be able to see spiritually, and that far transcends the blessing of earthly sight, precious as it is. It would be better by far not to see on earth than be plunged into the darkness of a lost eternity. To be raised from spiritual death is a greater miracle than Lazarus experienced at Bethany. He still had to put his personal faith in Christ if he was to enter heaven. There was little point in living a little longer on earth if he was to suffer eternal death. These are the "greater things" promised by Jesus, and witnessed by us. These signs in John's gospel are not only visible proofs of his deity but persuasive symbols of what he will do throughout history in the lives of believing men and women. We are privileged people if these miracles have happened in our own lives and we shall surely want to see them in the lives of others. Those who love the Father will want to share in the doing of "works" such as these, signs that will last for eternity.

Of course, there is always the danger that, in a triumphalist spirit, believers will attempt these "greater things" in their own strength, or in their own way, or with their own ideas. That is why, at this time, Jesus said important things to Philip about prayer. Disciples must "ask" for these "greater things".

Needing the Father's help

We have already seen that John's gospel maintains the perfect balance between Christ's unique deity and his essential humanity. One of the ways his human nature is underlined in these narratives is by means of Jesus' own repeated sayings about his total dependence on the Father. That is asserted both in the passage before us and elsewhere in the gospel. His words and his works come directly from God. But, in this gospel Jesus asks in prayer for those things he needs both for himself (11:41; 17:1–5) and for all who follow him (14:16; 17:6–26). He urges his disciples to do the same: "And I will do whatever you ask in my name . . . You may ask me for anything in my name, and I will do it" (13–14; 15:7, 16: 23–24, 26).

Jesus knows that his best disciples will constantly express their reliance on their Father. The words they speak derive from him, and the works they do are energized by him. Prayer is their life line. Every day they tell the Father how much they need him, and they make their requests "in the name" of Jesus. What does that mean exactly? It means four things – asking on his authority, for his will, in his strength, and to his glory.

To ask anything of the Father in the name of Jesus is to ask it on his authority. To do something in the ancient world in the name of somebody else meant that you were undertaking that task on their behalf. You were standing in for them, as it were. Their good name, status and influence was behind you as you took up the assignment. You were merely an instrument of their purposes. Something of that is surely in mind here when we are told to ask "in the name" of Jesus. We are to remember that when we come to the Father's throne it is because Jesus has exemplified our coming, told us to come, and has promised to meet us there. When we ask, we are asking with all his unique authority behind us.

When we request anything "in his name" we are also asking for his will. We are not demanding something for our own selfish ends. Praying "in his name" means consciously seeking only for those things he would be asking for us. It means discerning those things which are of the greatest spiritual importance, not for those which are of the greatest material benefit, or the greatest social significance. It means praying as Jesus did in Gethsemane's garden: "Not my will but yours be done" (Luke 22:42). It means that, like Jesus, we are wanting to know what will please the Father (5:30; 8:29) rather than what might satisfy us. It means having a right sense of priorities, and having the ability to discern that what might seem right for us is not always best for us.

I treasure a letter which I received over thirty years ago from Dr W. E. Sangster, the outstanding Methodist preacher. Without realizing that he was so desperately ill, I had written to ask for some initial advice about a research degree topic in an area of theological study which he knew well. A prompt letter back brought me the information I needed, and the sad news of his incurable illness. He was suffering from the rare disease of progressive muscular atrophy and could only speak with difficulty. Even that blessing was to be withdrawn from him as the weeks went by, and he was left only with the power to hold a pen between finger and thumb. For a man who had held thousands captive by magnificent oratory and sparkling exposition, it was suffering indeed.

At that time, I was a young minister in his first pastorate. I had admired him greatly, though from a distance. The concluding sentences of the letter came as a reminder from a dying man of what mattered most in life. These are the things to seek "in the name" of Christ:

> And now in my sickness I am grateful to God for his many mercies, glad there are useful things I can still do, and am ready for all his perfect will.

Virtually paralysed, he was unable to do the many things he had once done with such astonishing excellence – preaching, teaching, writing, caring for a huge congregation, leading the evangelistic endeavour of a major denomination. All that was gone, but the greatest things remained, and they are in that letter's conclusion – abundant gratitude, willing service, and total surrender. To pray "in his name" is voluntarily to limit ourselves to the priorities of Jesus.

When we make our requests "in his name" we are also asking in his strength. We are thereby confessing that prayer can never be effective if we attempt it in the power of our own severely limited physical and intellectual resources. We shall soon grow tired if we rely on our own energy. Our minds will quickly weary if our mental powers are all we can bring to the ministry of prayer. Those who pray "in his name" count on the resources of the promised Holy Spirit. He enlightens the mind and quickens the body.

Paul told the believers at Rome that those who count on his help will never be weary in prayer:

> ... the Spirit helps us in our weakness. We do not know what we ought to pray for, but the Spirit himself intercedes for us with groans that words cannot express. And he who searches our hearts knows the mind of the Spirit, because the Spirit intercedes for the saints in accordance with the will of God (Romans 8:26–27).

It is Paul's experience that when we come to the place of prayer, the Spirit helps us by praying *with* us, as Christ helps us by praying *for* us (Romans 8:34; Hebrews 7:25).

Supremely, to pray "in his name" is to ask "for his glory". It means seeking only those things which will exalt God, magnify Christ and honour the Spirit. It means deliberately directing the searchlight away from what may bring pleasure to us to what will bring joy to him. So, asking "for anything" in the name of Jesus means putting all those ambitious requests through this refining filter. It does not mean that whatever we want is ours for the asking. Even Jesus wondered whether that cup of suffering might be avoided, but he saw clearly that he could not hope to exalt the Father except by way of the Cross. The path of suffering became the route to glory.

Those disciples who share the priorities of Jesus reveal their love for the Father by the things they seek as well as by the things they do. The disciple's most earnest prayer is that the Father may be glorified. That is certainly how Jesus prayed. This brings us to the last of those five things which Jesus shared with his disciple on the day Philip asked to see the Father.

Seeking the Father's glory

The disciple's lifestyle, words, deeds and prayer need to be sharply focused on this single aim – to glorify the Father. That is how Jesus lived, served and prayed (17:1–5) and those who follow him must not be content with lesser ambitions. All too easily our service can be spoilt and our witness marred by selfish motives. The best things can be stained by the worst ambitions.

I know a church in southern England whose impressive tower was built through the generosity of one donor who paid for it to be erected in memory of his grandmother. But the kind thought is spoilt because the prominent memorial tablet exalts the donor instead of recalling his grandmother. We learn nothing whatever about her, and far more than we need about him. The benevolent act gave him a marvellous opportunity to say something helpful about his grandmother, but the grandson used it to say something special about himself. In embarrassing detail it describes his social status and wide achievements. The donor used the opportunity to exalt himself. It is a sad parable, and disciples do well to ponder it. Those who are truly Christ's followers refuse to parade themselves. They want to live like him – entirely to the glory of God.

When Jesus reached the end of his earthly life he longed that his Father might be glorified, even in the anguish of that cruel Cross. What had characterized his life from the beginning was manifest right until its close. The gifted Old Testament scholar, H. Wheeler Robinson, once put it like this: "The way in which a man begins a job shows what he will do with it; the way he finishes it shows what it has done with him." When Christ's work on earth was finishing, he found his greatest peace in the assurance that he had done everything in life to the glory of God, and now he was ending it that way too.

When earthly lives are at their inevitable end, the value of material things fades into insignificance. Social status, economic security, intellectual ability, academic honours, and professional skills, are of little value when we are on the threshold of eternity. What will matter then is whether we have glorified God on the earth. Even some believers are strangely dismissive about death. They consider it morbid to give it consideration when life is buoyant and bright and exciting. Time for all that much later. But it's strange for a Christian to banish the topic when Jesus had important things to say about it. R. D. Blackmore reminds us of the most important things when we reach that moment:

> In the hour of death, after this life's whim,
> When the heart beats low, and the eyes grow dim,
> And the pain has exhausted every limb –
> The lover of the Lord shall trust in Him.
>
> When the will has forgotten the lifelong aim,
> And the mind can only disgrace its fame,
> And a man is uncertain of his own name –
> The power of the Lord shall fill this frame.
>
> For even the purest delight may pall,
> And power must fade, and the pride must fall,
> And the love of the dearest friends grow small –
> But the glory of the Lord is all in all.[3]

"The glory of the Lord" – all the great New Testament leaders join with the Christ they loved in urging us to make his glory our greatest aim. Paul weaves the theme into all his letters so that the early Christian people realize its importance in everyday living (Romans 11:36; 15:17;

16:27). Peter insists that every act of Christian speaking or serving will be matched by the strength we need, but it must be done for the glory of God, not for the praise of men (1 Peter 4:10–11). In John's graphic anticipation of heaven, nothing is of greater importance than the glorified Lord, and the exultant multitude of true worshippers who sing, "To him be glory and power for ever and ever" (Revelation 1:6; 4:9, 11; 5:12, 13; 7:12; 11:13; 14:7; 19:1; 21:11, 23).

Disciples on earth strive for nothing less. The narrow span of human life is their unique opportunity to honour God. They pray with their Master: "it was for this reason I came to this hour. Father, glorify your name!" (12:27–28).

1 John Foxe, *Acts and Monuments* (popularly known as *The Book of Martyrs*), 1563, ed. S. R. Cattley and George Townsend, 1837–41, Vol. IV, 635

2 Floyd McClung, Jr and Kalafi Moala, *Nine Worlds to Win*, Word UK Ltd 1989, 15–16

3 R. D. Blackmore, "Dominus Illuminatio Mea"